Mike's a quality person, and he's a leader. Mike expresses his faith daily, both on and off the field, by example.

Ray Agnew—defensive tackle, St. Louis Rams

In one glorious moment, Mike Jones wrote his way into football history. For the first time ever, people will talk about "The Tackle." He also has a wonderful reputation, and he represents it well.

Jack Buck—longtime baseball and football broadcaster

They say good things happen to good people, and Mike Jones is one of the "good people." St. Louis has been blessed with some tremendous athletes who do great work both on and off the field, but I've never come across any athlete who cares more about his community than Mike Jones.

Mike Bush—Sports Director for KSDK-TV (NBC), St. Louis

I think Mike was truly the unsung hero on this team this year. If you ask me who I'd want next to me at outside linebacker, I'd take him any day, over anybody. Michael never wavers. I don't care where it is—on the field, off the field, in the weight room, in the locker room—he's always that great person, always that faithful person, who's always there. He's just an unbelievable man—someone I definitely pattern myself after.

Kevin Carter—defensive end, St. Louis Rams

Long before "making the play that saved the day" in Super Bowl XXXIV, Michael Jones was a champion. His efforts on behalf of charities throughout the St. Louis region are the hallmark of a true winner. United Way lauds his accomplishments because on and off the field he is helping children achieve their dreams.

Charmaine S. Chapman—President and Chief Executive Officer, United Way of Greater St. Louis

Beyond being an outstanding football player, Mike Jones is one of the classiest athletes I've ever run across. It's not often that a professional athlete adopts a new hometown like Mike has. The Michael Jones Foundation is an invaluable asset to the entire community. On the field, he's the kind of player that always seems to be in the right place at the right time. And he knows his opponent and can explain what another team does or why something happened. In fact, his knowledge of the opposition is probably the primary reason he was in place to make The Tackle. Jones' play certainly goes down as one of my top five moments in sports. His book, and his story, is a must read for any fan interested in what professional football should be.

Randy Karraker—sports broadcaster with KMOX Radio, St. Louis

It was a fitting end to a dream season—Mike Jones, a native son of Missouri, making "the hit" to win the world championship. Of the many wonderful, quality individuals we had playing for the Rams on that team, Mike was the epitome of excellence. Mike is an outstanding leader both on and off the field. It's those qualities that led him to make the play that will go down in history.

Stan Kroenke—part-owner, St. Louis Rams

For years, Mike Jones has been dedicated to helping the kids of Missouri and Illinois through his charitable foundation. He was a hero long before he made the greatest defensive play in Super Bowl history. Thanks to one of the nation's best football writers, Jim Thomas, fans can now get a close, personal look at this compassionate, community-minded man who is definitely an MVP—most valuable player and person.

Bernie Miklasz—sports columnist for the
St. Louis Post-Dispatch

As players, we know what kind of person Michael is, what he does in the community. He is such a leader, not only by example, but vocally. He's the ultimate role model. He has a great work ethic—on and off the field. He's a wonderful human being. He's the kind of guy that you want your son to grow up to be like.

Ricky Proehl—wide receiver, St. Louis Rams

Making the Play

The Inspirational Story of Mike Jones

as told to Jim Thomas
of the *St. Louis Post-Dispatch*

CPH

SAINT LOUIS

Concordia Publishing House staff includes—
Editor: Dawn Mirly Weinstock
Production Coordinator/Print Buyer: Mary Lou Kopp
Cover design: Jared Neisler
Book design: Melissa Jarnagin

Published by Concordia Publishing House
3558 S. Jefferson Avenue, St. Louis, MO 63118-3968

Manufactured in the United States of America

1 2 3 4 5 6 7 8 9 10   09 08 07 06 05 04 03 02 01 00

Contents

Foreword

Coach Dick Vermeil

(Head Coach of the St. Louis Rams,
1997–1999 and 1999 NFL Coach of the Year)

Mike Jones might very well have made the most famous, widely renowned tackle in the history of the National Football League. Since that tackle, since that game, almost daily, I'm asked about not only the play, but the person involved who stepped up and made the play. By now, I've gotten my response down pretty well, but I'm not sure if people truly buy into what I say. My routine answer is *I'm not surprised Mike made that great play because rising to the highest level is what he is all about.* In fact, I've said many times, if I were going to select one person on defense with the game in the balance, I would select Mike to determine my own and my team's fate. He's all about being at the right place at the right time.

Now why would I say that? First, Mike Jones made a number of plays over the course of our season that were more difficult and required more athletic ability to make than that final play. It was the magnitude of the Super Bowl, the time in the game, and the area on the field in which the play took place that made it appear to be unusually spectacular. Second, that kind of play fits Mike Jones' personal profile to the tee. He's a winner and winners make championship plays! Everything he does, everything he is, on and off the field, is embodied in that tackle.

I've always believed people ultimately demonstrate who they are by what they do, and the last play of the Super Bowl gave millions of people the opportunity to see what I mean. Mike believes in what he does and does what he believes. He unselfishly gives of himself to all those he connects with, and that is why he will always be successful. In fact, as a football coach you have to be very careful not to overlook all Mike Jones brings to the table because he does what he's supposed to do, and therefore, is easy to take for granted. I personally really tried hard not to allow this to happen. I can't tell you how many times I've told Mike he is very special. The fact that he won the Carl Ekern Spirit Award three years in a row and was voted Defensive Captain as well tells you that his teammates felt the same as I do. He's just a special human being!

One of the greatest things a person can be is a good example to all those he comes in contact with, and Mike really showed everybody what they should be—persistent. Mike is very persistent! He came out of college a running back, and the Raiders converted him to an outside linebacker position, even sending him to play one year in the World League. As I put my staff together in 1997, I hired Mike White, who had just finished his tenure as the Raiders' head coach. It was Coach White who encouraged me to bring Mike Jones to St. Louis. He was a free agent at that time. Coach White believed Mike Jones' best football was ahead of him, and he knew how much more he would bring to the locker room in the way of personal leadership. Boy, was he ever right on! Although we continued to lose our first two seasons, Mike Jones' stability was really a big leadership factor in keeping us together as we went through those tough times.

Because players knew I had tremendous respect for Mike, they would send him to my office with special requests. Normally, the request centered around practice tempo, full pads, curfew, and free time. Despite my reputation for doing things my way, more often than not I found myself going along with Mike. Why? Because I trusted his judgment in certain things even more than my own. He had the pulse of the team in his hands, and I knew he would never abuse his leadership role nor sacrifice mine.

I think by now you can surmise that I appreciate the opportunity to publicly share my respect for Mike Jones. Mike is all about making a difference. The personally organized and administered Michael Jones Foundation is a perfect example of what I've been trying to put into words. Mike makes as many big plays off the field as he does under big-game conditions. I'll be very surprised if you don't come away with the same feelings about the football player and the human being after you read this compelling story!

Foreword

Clarence R. Stephenson Sr.

(Longtime friend and mentor and former coach of Mike Jones and former player for the Kansas City Monarchs)

Working in the sports field, one can never foresee the impact of teaching fundamentals of sports to a young athlete.

In the middle 1970s, I had the opportunity to coach my son's Little League team. That was the beginning of what I know now was an interaction with a future sports star, Mike Jones, who has made a significant contribution to National Football League history.

Several characteristics seen during Mike's childhood clearly defined his attitude. As a youth, he always showed the determination to succeed and be the best because finishing second never seemed acceptable.

At the age of 10, Mike became a participant in the National Collegiate Athletic Association's (NCAA) National Youth Summer Sports Program. The NYSSP was designed to teach boys and girls, ages 10 to 18, sports skills. As a part of this program, Mike learned how to correctly perform skills he continues to use today. To participate in the program, Mike had to have a physical, which was offered free by the University of Missouri in Kansas City. These free physicals allowed Mike to play sports in the Interscholastic League [the Kansas City school league] during his formative school years. Being a part of the summer sports program instilled the confidence that he could compete against anyone. In both Little League baseball and football, Mike played a vital roll in leading our teams to championships through his last-inning hits or game-winning touchdowns.

After participating in the summer program for six years, Mike became an employee of the National Youth Summer Sports Program. His work experience began as a kitchen helper, cleaning tables, serving food, and performing other duties as assigned. The following year, I noticed his leadership abilities and promoted Mike to assistant group leader. Eventually he became a squad leader, working with the 10-year-old boys as they learned basic sports skills.

A turning point in Mike's life came during the summer of his sixteenth year. Mike came to talk to me about buying his first car. He expressed to me that if he bought a car he would no longer want to play ball. I told him that it would be fine, but he would need to look for other employment because he would no longer be working for me. With his mother's support, he decided to continue to work and play ball.

Through his experiences, I feel Mike became successful. They also gave him the desire to give back to the community. When Mike became a member of the Oakland Raiders organization, he always stayed in touch with me and many times sought my advice. When he felt it was time to make a move and relocate, he consulted with me. The advice I gave is one reason Mike is a member of the St. Louis Rams today.

Many of the young sports talents I had the opportunity to teach or coach have moved on to play professional football, baseball, or basketball. Mike's development of skills as an athlete, his dedication, the respect shown to his friends and family, as well as his contributions to the community as an outstanding citizen have proven that a professional athlete can achieve balance. One reward for his dedication and passion is the opportunity to sit back, relax, and humbly enjoy his successes with those around him.

I want to thank Mike's mother and father for sharing their son's growth and success with me. Indeed, it has been more than a pleasure.

Acknowledgments

Covering a professional sports team on a daily basis isn't always as glamorous as it may seem to the "outsider." The hours are long and the days off are rare. So when approached by Concordia Publishing House about writing a biography of Mike Jones, I initially had mixed feelings. The late spring and early summer months represent "down" time for an NFL writer—a rare opportunity to unwind, spend time with family, and recharge for the next season.

But I had covered Mike's entire career at the University of Missouri, when Tiger football and basketball were my beat. I had watched him score a touchdown with a broken hand against Indiana and seen him toting his firstborn daughter, Taelor, around the Tigers' practice facility. At the professional level, I have covered every game—and nearly every practice—in which Mike has participated since signing a free-agent contract with the St. Louis Rams in 1997.

In short, no other writer has seen as much of Mike's career. So it just fit. Besides, I have always admired the way Mike carries himself on and off the football field. Working on this book only deepened my admiration for him. At a time when off-the-field problems have become a major issue in the NFL, Mike's story needed to be told.

I would like to thank the love of my life, my wife, Paula, and my three sons—Timothy, Jonathan, and Roger—for their help and their patience with this project. Also, thanks to my mother, Effie; sisters, Corinne, Elizabeth, and Christine; and Uncle Nick Ballta for always being there.

Thanks also to my colleagues in the *Post-Dispatch* sports department, including my brother, Stephan. In his own quiet, low-key way, he is *my* hero.

Dawn Mirly Weinstock, Managing Editor at Concordia Publishing House, is a consummate professional. Matt Small of the *Kansas City Star* went beyond the call of duty in assisting in research on Stacy Simpson.

Finally, I would like to dedicate this book to the memory of my late father, Nick S. Thomas— a kind, hardworking man, whose time came too soon.

Jim Thomas

Making the Play

The Inspirational Story of Mike Jones

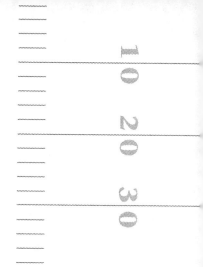

1

A Wing and a Prayer

At the end of the usual Super Bowl halftime extravaganza, hundreds of doves—Styrofoam doves—floated down from the roof of the Georgia Dome. "They fell just on our side. I don't know why they picked our side," Mary Jo Jones says.

Mary Jo believes doves—even Styrofoam ones—are a Christian symbol, a symbol of the Holy Spirit. *"I've got to get a dove! Jan, get me one!"* she remembers calling out.

Try as she might, Jan—Mary Jo's daughter—couldn't get one. Finally, she jumped and grabbed the last dove as it floated down. With a black marker, Jan wrote on its wings: *No. 52. Mike Jones.* That's her kid brother and Mary Jo's son. He plays linebacker for the St. Louis Rams.

Mary Jo held that last dove for most of the second half. Before the last play of Super Bowl XXXIV, Mary Jo put down the dove and grabbed Jan's hands. The twosome turned away from the field, faced each other, and prayed.

"We prayed to the Holy Spirit," Mary Jo says. " 'Enlighten us, God. And strengthen us,' we prayed. Those are some of the things that you ask the Holy Spirit to do."

So they weren't watching the final play of the Super Bowl. "The next thing I know, I heard everybody screaming," Jan remembers. "I said, 'Momma, what happened?' "

But Mary Jo didn't know what had happened either. But a couple seats away, Mike's wife, Leslie, had been watching the play unfold. She saw Tennessee quarterback Steve McNair drop back to pass. "We saw McNair throw the ball," Leslie recalls. "We saw somebody catch the ball. And at that point, we couldn't see anything else."

Because at that precise moment, one of those movable TV camera cranes had obstructed her view.

In a different section of the stadium not far away, Kevin Jones—one of Mike's older brothers—broke tradition. Normally, he watches Mike no matter what the score or game circumstance. But he couldn't help himself this time. With the Rams clinging to a 23–16 lead, with 6 seconds left in football's biggest game, with Tennessee on the Rams' 10-yard line, he looked away from where Mike was lining up in the Rams' defensive formation.

"I was watching the ball," Kevin confesses. "I was watching McNair and Eddie George. It all happened so fast—it was like 'Boom! Boom! Boom!' "

In Columbia, Missouri, David Johnson was watching the game at his brother-in-law's house. There were about 20 other people watching too. "When that pass was thrown, it looked like that guy was going in for the touchdown," Johnson says. "Because no one was in the picture at that time for the Rams. And then out of the clear blue sky, this person from the Rams comes in and makes this incredible tackle."

Actually, along came Mike Jones. Mike tackled Titans wide receiver Kevin Dyson about 1½ yards—maybe 50 inches—from the goal line as time expired.

"So you're excited about that, and then as the Rams' player gets up you see the number," says Johnson, who has done charity work with Mike. "And it's Mike Jones! I think my head hit the ceiling."

In Kansas City, Keith Hannaman and his wife had returned home early from a Super Bowl party. They had sent the baby-sitter home. Hannaman's wife was doing the laundry. He turned on the television to watch the final moments of the game. Mike made the play, and Hannaman went absolutely bonkers.

"I went beserk," says Hannaman, Mike's high school football coach. "Jumping up and down, screaming, yelling, practically doing cartwheels. And I look up, and there's my 8-year-old daughter, Jessica, coming out of her bedroom. She walks right past me, looks at the TV, looks at me, and says, 'Daddy, that's not Penn State. Why are you acting like that?' "

Once a walk-on wide receiver for Penn State, Hannaman normally reserves such hysterics for Nittany Lions football. "Well, sweetie, this is just about as important to me as Penn State," he remembers telling his daughter.

Watching at home in East Lansing, Michigan, Mike Ward didn't know who had made the stop at first. Then he saw the Rams' tackler roll over and saw the jersey: Jones, 52. Ward turned to his wife. *"That's a play that will go down in the ages,"* he told her.

There are few football fans in the world as qualified as Ward to make such a statement. As a youngster, he was a ballboy for Vince Lombardi, the legendary football coach of the Green Bay Packers. He was at the "Ice Bowl" when Bart Starr scored on a quarterback sneak to give the Packers a 21–17 victory over Dallas in the legendary 1967 NFL championship game.

"So I know what plays go down in the ages," Ward says. "And Mike's play, it hit me in the same vein. It struck me in the same way. I got chills at that point and was just excited for him."

NFL history has other examples of such heroics and such memorable games. But "The Catch," and "The Drive," and the Ice Bowl, and many others must now make room for "The Tackle." Because with the game on the line, Mike Jones made the greatest defensive play in Super Bowl history, capping one of the most memorable Super Bowl games ever.

It couldn't have happened to a more unassuming player. Undrafted out of college, Mike had nothing handed to him as an NFL player. "He earned it. And earned it in a very unique way," says Ward, once Mike's running backs coach at the University of Missouri. "I have a lot of respect for that."

Mike didn't earn a starting job until his fifth NFL season. Long before that, he served an apprenticeship in the World League. Forty linebackers were selected by NFL teams in the 1991 college draft. Most have long since faded from the scene.

"Mike's had a good, solid career of fulfillment and purpose," says Oakland Raiders owner Al Davis, who signed Mike to his first NFL contract. "I just hope that he enjoys a great life.

With us, the door will always be open for him."

Mike doesn't have a flashy nickname. He doesn't have a flashy style of play. He doesn't really pile up the flashy stats.

"He's not like an 'LT'—a great blitz guy coming off the edge," Rams defensive coordinator Peter Giunta says. (The reference, of course, being to former Giants great Lawrence Taylor.)

But for nearly a decade now, Mike has carved out a productive career through perseverance and hard work. Mike is a foot soldier. He's an ordinary man possessing some extraordinary qualities. It wasn't a fluke or mere happenstance that he was in the right place at the right time at the end of Super Bowl XXXIV. And the approach he takes on the football field is the same approach he takes in life.

"You like to see guys like Mike make those kind of plays," says Hall of Fame safety Ronnie Lott, one of Mike's former teammates. "Guys that are good guys. Guys that have worked hard and finally get that moment to shine, to have the spotlight put on them. It comes from preparation, but it also comes from 'want-to.' "

Not to diminish Mike's athletic skills, which are abundant, but there are many better players in the NFL than Mike Jones. But very few players have as much "want-to" as Mike. "Mike Jones demonstrates what he is by what he does," says Dick Vermeil, former Rams head coach. "Just watch what he does. Everything that he does. It defines him. He doesn't have to say much. He puts what he is into action.

"And he's not a big conversationalist. He's not quite as bashful and shy as a lot of people think. Basically, I would classify him as slightly shy. And maybe even a better description than shy is very sincere."

Sincere in his approach to football. Sincere in his approach to others. Sincere in his religious beliefs. Sincere in his commitment to community service. He was this way long before he became famous for The Tackle.

Take his early years in the NFL with the Raiders. Mike eagerly volunteered for charity work and public appearances, even though some organizations privately asked the Raiders' public relations office, *"Uh, could you send Tim Brown instead?"*

At his first free football camps in St. Louis, it wasn't uncommon for kids to walk up right up to him and ask: *"Okay, which one is Mike Jones?"*

"I'm Mike Jones," Mike would reply to the astonishment of the youngsters.

Mike doesn't put on airs, seek attention, or attempt to be something he's not. "He's very genuine," Ward says.

"What you see with Michael is Michael," his

wife, Leslie, says. "He's not putting on anything. He's very quiet if he doesn't know you. He doesn't talk a lot. He has to get his own comfort zone with people."

So why are all these people raving about Mike Jones? Why were they so happy to see him make The Tackle? And what did they have to do with his development as a player, a person, a husband, a father, a Christian?

Read on.

But we'll let Ward reveal part of the story line. "This is about Mike Jones and his will to make it happen," Ward says. "It's about his drive. And it's about his faith and his belief in God. That's his strength, his conviction. And it's about his will to endure. And that's what he's done. He has not quit. He stayed with it."

Mike stayed with it through ups and downs, highs and lows, successes and setbacks, trials and tribulations. Everyone who's ever been a foot soldier can appreciate his story.

Oh, by the way. That Styrofoam dove hangs prominently in the Kansas City home of Mary Jo and Leroy Jones—Mike's parents. It hangs right next to a picture of Jesus.

2

A Solid Foundation

Fundamentally perfect. That's how the football experts describe Mike Jones. All you have to do is look to his childhood and his parents to see where his work ethic, Christian faith, strong belief in family, and dedication to the community come from. And perhaps Mike's tenacity and interest in community concerns connect him even further back—to his maternal grandparents.

Leading the Fight

There was a grade school across the street from Mary Josephine Baker's home in Pleasant Hill, Missouri. But it was for the white folks. Blacks had to go to a different school. And at this school, there were only two teachers for everyone—grades 1 through 8. Segregation was at its worst in America, and in this part of western Missouri, it was a case of separate but unequal schools for blacks and whites.

"At the black school they didn't have running water—no water faucets," Mary Jo says. "Tuberculosis was running rampant down there. My mother went to Jefferson City and protested."

Mary Jo's mother (Mike Jones' grandmother), Neosha, was ahead of her time—fighting for civil rights in the late 1930s and early '40s. "Her father was kind of like a politician—and he taught a lot of that to Momma—the rights and everything like that," Mary Jo recalls. "She knew that school kids had to have equal. They could have separate but equal, but they weren't getting equal."

Neosha's trip to the state capital in Jefferson City eventually helped the school get water fountains, but she wanted more than a better school for her children. Neosha wanted a better community atmosphere in which to raise her family. So the family moved west to Kansas City in 1941. Mary Jo's father stayed in Pleasant Hill, commuting to Kansas City on his off days to be with the family.

Like most parents, the Bakers wanted their children to be better off than they were. The move to the city gave the children the opportunity to attend better schools—and an education opened many doors, as Mary Jo's father knew from experience.

"My dad was an electrical engineer," Mary Jo says. "He started out shoveling coal. I'll tell you what happened: He took correspondence courses to learn trigonometry and geometry, and he taught himself. He worked himself up."

William and Neosha both believed God gives each person unique gifts to use in service of others. William worked hard to develop his gift, eventually garnering the attention of his employer, Missouri Public Service.

William Baker devised a way to stoke a furnace in a cost-efficient way using less coal. His employer was so impressed that they asked him to show the process he devised to students from what is now called the University of Missouri—Rolla.

Once in Kansas City, the Baker family left the Methodist church and converted to Catholicism in 1947, right around the time the Kansas City Catholic schools began to integrate. Mary Jo transferred from a public high school to a Catholic school—Glennon High—before her junior year. She was the first black student ever to attend Glennon.

"Here in Kansas City, we never had to ride in the back of the bus," Mary Jo says. "It was mixed all over the city. There was white and black all over the city. I see a lot of people that I know are younger than I am—they speak about when they rode in the back of the bus. But I don't remember it."

That didn't prevent Mary Jo from being subjected to racism at Glennon. "That first day, there were some kids outside the school yelling something like, 'Chocolate pudding! Chocolate cake!' when I walked by," she recalls. "But they were kids that didn't go to the school. They were kids that lived in the neighborhood, and they had heard that there was going to be some integration.

"We didn't have it bad at Glennon. At Lillis [Catholic] High School they had it hard. Two of my best girlfriends went to Lillis. Both were very light-skinned, but in the yearbook their pictures were so dark you couldn't even make out who they were." It was as if the yearbook editors wanted everyone to know that Jean and Doris—Mary Jo's friends—were black.

Neosha Baker had some simple words of advice on the subject for Mary Jo. "My momma just said, 'Ignore it. You've got to be above it,' " Mary Jo remembers.

Leroy and Mary Jo

Leroy Jones Sr. was born in 1932 in the tiny town of Franklin, just outside Pittsburg, Kansas. When Leroy was about 6 years old, his parents separated and both moved to Kansas City.

Leroy spent periods of time with his mother in the city, but lived with his grandparents. His grandfather was a sharecropper, who raised wheat and corn on a small spread.

In the fifth grade, Leroy went to live in the city with his mother. Just as he had while living on the farm, Leroy continued to play baseball and basketball with friends.

Leroy graduated as valedictorian of his class from a vocational school—Coles High in Kansas City—when he was only 16. (As sometimes happened at this period of time, Leroy was able to skip the eighth grade.) He wasn't Catholic, but a friend from the neighborhood—Donald Caldwell—was, so Leroy began tagging along with Donald and some other friends to church functions.

"Back in those days, they didn't have but one or two Catholic churches here, and the black Catholic church was St. Joseph's," Mary Jo says. "The CYC—Catholic Youth Council—would meet on Tuesday nights, and they had dances, and parties, and stuff like that. We'd play games, have fun, and pray.

"It was just for teenagers. Leroy wasn't Catholic at the time, but you know how boys angle into things." Especially when girls are involved.

Now, we'd like to say that it was love at

first sight, but that would be incorrect. Did Mary Jo notice Leroy right off the bat? "No," she says. "He got my telephone number, and the first time he called, he acted like he was another guy."

When he called, Leroy pretended to be Fred Harvey, one of his buddies. This could have been a practical joke, a case of shyness, or a combination of both. But the effort was wasted on Mary Jo Baker. "I didn't know either one of them," she remembers.

But Leroy kept attending those Tuesday night functions. So did Mary Jo. "And we just kind of paired up," Mary Jo says. They were married on February 23, 1952. Fred Harvey was the best man.

Family Times

Leroy and Mary Jo Jones wasted little time starting a family. Patti was born in '52. She still lives in Kansas City and works as a consultant. Her specialty is writing grant applications for nonprofit groups and performing artists. And in case you think Mike Jones received all the athletic talent in the family, you'd be very wrong. All the Jones children have enjoyed sports. Patti was a stellar track and field athlete in high school and attended Creighton University in Omaha, Nebraska, where she continued to play club sports.

In 1953, Leroy Jr. came along. He was a talented baseball player in his time, and now he works as an airline mechanic in Orlando, Florida. The family calls him Flipper because of his early adoration of the TV dolphin.

In 1956, a second girl was born—Jan. She was quite the softball pitcher as a teenager and now lives in Kansas City where she works as a dispatcher for a bus company.

In 1957, the birth of Kevin seemed to signal a "complete" family of two boys and two girls. He was a star track athlete and football player in high school and has worked as a firefighter in Kansas City for the last 23 years. He's now assigned to the hazardous materials unit of the Kansas City Fire Department.

After Kevin's birth, family life settled down for the Joneses. Mary Jo continued to pursue a career in the civil service, which she entered right out of high school. After taking time to raise her children and time off for a couple major illnesses, Mary Jo retired in 1994 after working for 23 years for the Department of the Treasury, the U.S. Postal Service, and the Internal Revenue Service. Leroy worked for Remington Rand (an office equipment manufacturer), then began a 32-year career as a mail clerk with the post office in 1965. He retired in 1997.

Roots II

The years rolled by. Patti, Leroy Jr., Jan, and Kevin grew up. Then something entirely unexpected happened. More than 11 years after Kevin's birth, Mary Jo discovered she was pregnant again! "I was very surprised," she says. "I thought I was through."

On tax day—April 15, 1969—Mary Jo gave birth to a healthy baby boy. Her mother, Neosha, came to St. Joseph's Hospital to visit her daughter and grandson.

"What'd you name him?" Neosha asked Mary Jo.

"K.C. Jones, Momma," Mary Jo said proudly.

Awkward moments followed.

"Here I was—34 years old," Mary Jo now recalls. "My momma can't pressure me." Right?

Wrong.

"You're not going to name him K.C. Jones. That's not a proper name," Neosha said.

Mary Jo now says, "Momma didn't force anything on us. She just put it in a way ..." that made you do it. The newest addition to the family left the hospital as Michael Anthony Jones. And he left wearing a little Kansas City A's baseball outfit—a birthday present from teenage brother Flipper, who was working at Municipal Stadium selling peanuts.

And Mike was not the last baby Mary Jo

had—not by a long shot. Michael was followed by baby sisters Kim (1970), Monica (1971), Maria (1973), and a baby brother, Mark (1975).

Mike's three younger sisters live in Kansas City, where Kim and Maria work as accountants and Monica works for a communications company. Mark lives in Columbia, Missouri.

In case you think Mike got the last of the athletic skill, you'd be wrong. All four of Mike's younger siblings played high school sports. For a time, the family thought Mark would be even better in football than Mike because he was bigger than his older brother.

If you do the math, there was a 12-year gap between the first group of four children and the second group of five—which the Jones family refers to as Roots II. Some friends and relatives joke that the Joneses must have gotten a new mattress or Leroy Sr. got his work shift changed, thus prompting the second wave of children that began with Mike.

"It wasn't planned. Didn't change shifts," Leroy Sr. says with a shrug. "It happened. I always wanted a big family because there were just two of us—me and my sister—and she died when she was 29."

A Big Family

At last count Leroy and Mary Jo, parents of

nine children, had 29 grandchildren and five great-grandchildren. The desire for a big family definitely has been realized.

What was it like raising nine children? "It wasn't with food stamps," Mary Jo says. "You didn't eat out. You cooked food at home." But on payday, the family would splurge and make a run to Dairy Queen for an ice-cream cone or a banana split.

"The kids liked to see me have babies," Mary Jo remembers. "When I went to the hospital to have babies, Daddy would take them out to eat. Daddy didn't do any cooking. Daddy took them out."

Raising nine children wasn't quite as hectic as you might think because the first group were all teenagers, or close to it (Kevin was 12), when Mike and his younger siblings came along. "They were old enough to baby-sit and help me out," Mary Jo says.

Mary Jo and Leroy enjoyed their children and were involved in all facets of their lives. Perhaps taking a page from her mother's book, Mary Jo was active in the school board and in the PTA at St. Augustine's Catholic School, which Mike and his siblings attended. The entire family went to church there as well, which was an every Sunday event.

"I never had any trouble [getting the kids

ready]," Mary Jo recalls. "It was an automatic thing. When Sunday came around, it was time to go to church."

From his family, Mike learned the importance of strong family connections, of education, of taking responsibility, of using the talents God gives you to the fullest, of seeing His faithful hand in the struggles and successes of life, and of working for the good of the community. He saw his parents committed to providing for their growing family and encouraging each child to develop to his or her fullest potential.

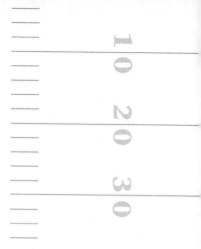

3

Mike "K.C." Jones

Kevin Jones isn't one of those firefighters who hesitates. He's been the first one in at hundreds of fires, but in nearly a quarter century with the Kansas City Fire Department, he has never been seriously injured on the job. "I guess God was looking out for me," he says.

Kevin made every one of Mike's Rams games in 1999, except for a December 26 home game against Chicago. It happened to be Kevin's turn to work the holiday shift. He and his fellow workers at Station No. 27 pulled some children from a fire on Christmas Day. The parents died. Kevin and his coworkers got some TV time, but it was a hollow moment.

"The little boy I pulled out was the same age as my grandbaby—3 years old," says Kevin. "He felt like my grandbaby does when I carry him into the bedroom at night. He felt just like him."

The Baby of the Family

That little boy Kevin rescued probably felt like his kid brother Mike did nearly 30 years ago when Kevin picked him up. For 12 years, Kevin had enjoyed being the baby of the family. "But I wanted some more brothers and sisters to play with," Kevin says. And his wish was fulfilled when Mike came along.

Mike Jones was only 8 months old when he began walking—out of necessity. He'd had an allergic reaction to penicillin that caused the skin on his knees to peel. "He was crawling around, and he probably couldn't take it anymore," Kevin remembers. "So he started to get up and walk."

Almost as soon as Mike could walk, he started playing games. "By the time summertime rolled around, he was walking good," Kevin recalls. "Me and him, we'd be out in that front yard with the baseball bat. He'd be going, 'Ball! Ball! Ball! Ball!' I'd pitch him that ball, and he'd start cranking them out in the street."

A couple of years later, Kevin and Mike began working on football. Kevin taught Mike to take handoffs in the living room of the family home on 76th Street in Kansas City. "He took a handoff one day and put his head down and ran," Kevin says. "He rammed me in my stomach so hard, he about knocked me down." Kevin was a sophomore in high school; Mike was around 3.

There was more to all this attention than a simple case of brotherly love. Kevin had a cousin named Walter, who was about 15 years old at this time, just like Kevin. And Walter had a kid brother named Eddie, who was about 3 at the time—just like Mike.

"It was like a competition," Mike says. "It was like Eddie and I were their little toys. They'd see who could run the fastest or could catch the ball the quickest." Or was best at taking handoffs.

Whatever the motive, Kevin's instruction had a lasting impact on Mike. Today, when Kevin works at one of Mike's charity football camps, he usually works with the youngest age group of kids. And he usually teaches them how to take handoffs.

Timeout or Playtime?

In addition to being very coachable, Mike had another character trait he often exhibited around the house—he was almost punishment proof. Not that Mary Jo, his mother, didn't try to make Mike understand the consequences of sassing or bopping one of his younger sisters. She often would send him to his room.

But Mike handled his punishment very well. When he was sent to his room, he wouldn't sulk;

instead, he would unleash his imagination and creativity. He'd take a deck of playing cards and make up sports games. Imaginary baseball. Imaginary football. Imaginary basketball. Imaginary track and field.

If he didn't have a deck of playing cards, Mike would use business cards. Or Monopoly money. Or even plain paper.

The exact rules of these games remain somewhat of a family mystery. "It was very complicated," Kevin says. "He'd say, 'That's my offense. This is my defense. We're going to run this play.'"

"I had it down to a science," Mike admits. "I would get a piece of paper and a pencil and play a full season. I would make up some imaginary teams. I'd have standings."

And Mike's imaginary teams previewed his later involvement in sports. "And I'd always have one team that was supposed to be the great team and another team that was the underdog," Mike recalls. "It always seemed like the team with less recognition always won."

Mike was so much into his imaginary games, his devotion to them would sometimes fluster his mother when she'd come to his room to inform him that punishment time was over and he could go outside and play. To her bewilderment, Mike often preferred to stay indoors—

at least for a while—to finish the imaginary game.

The Start of a Career

So you don't think Mike spent all of his time in his room, most of his games were the real kind played outdoors. Mike began playing organized baseball in the first grade as a member of the St. Augustine's Little League team. In Mike's second season with the team, they lost their first game. But St. Augustine's ran the table for the next few years—not losing a single game. Mike played catcher and hammered the ball as a hitter. He was so good at the national pastime at this early age that some members of his family thought his future was in baseball—not football.

Mike didn't begin playing organized "tackle" football until the fifth grade, somewhat against the wishes of his mother. "I didn't want him to play football," Mary Jo says. "Football was too rough."

One of the most influential coaches in Mike's early development was Clarence Stephenson, a former Negro League baseball player with the Kansas City Monarchs. "He showed me the way to do different things as far as football and baseball," Mike says. "And beyond that, he showed me how to be a good human being."

Stephenson coached many of Mike's Little League baseball and football teams. He also was director of a youth sports program, and as Mike got older, he began working with Stephenson as a youth coach. Mike and his friends spent a lot of time at the rec center with Stephenson.

"In the summertime, we'd stay there all day with him," Mike says. "Then we'd go play baseball. Sometimes we'd spend the night over at his house. He was like a surrogate father for a lot of guys that I grew up with."

For every organized game, Mike and his neighborhood friends played dozens of unorganized games. There was basketball in Mrs. Hart's backyard. There were activities at the youth center. Most of all, there was the broad median on Paseo Boulevard, just down the block from the Jones home. This green island served as the unofficial home "stadium" for dozens of preteens in Kansas City when Mike was in his "Wonder Bread" years.

Mike and his friends played baseball, football, and even basketball at the median. The tree line on either side served as the out-of-bounds markers, effectively preventing the players from going out in the street. For a basketball "court," Mike and his friends used a wire coat hanger to fashion a makeshift basket on an old tree in the middle of the median. Groups from different parts of the Paseo median formed "teams" to play their neighbors in pickup games. Mike's 76th Street group would take on a squad from 78th Street, and so on.

The competition was fierce, and this was the spawning ground for some of the top prep and college athletes in Kansas City at the time. Mike recalls more than a dozen all-state high school athletes, in a variety of sports, who grew up playing on the Paseo median. Some of them became his best friends: Arthur Armstrong. Darren Fulcher. Marvin Fight. Vincent Lee. But no one was a better friend than Kenny White.

Mike and Kenny

Young Kenny White would stay with his grandmother, who lived across the street from the Jones house, until his parents picked him up after work. "He was like my first best friend," Mike says. "I met him when I was like 3 years old. Every person that I met, Kenny met. The first things I did, I had to do it with him."

Mike and Kenny went all the way through grade school and high school together, except for a couple of years. They played their first organized baseball and football together. When they were running backs at Southwest High, teammates and even coaches would occasionally tease Mike with, *"Hey, Mike, if you don't start running hard, Kenny's going to replace you."*

"Everybody loved to be around Kenny," Mike recalls. "He was fun. He would crack jokes. He was a great guy. He had a great personality. People would gravitate to him." Years later, trouble would gravitate to Kenny in a way that affected the rest of Mike Jones' adult life. But all in all, it was a blissful childhood for Mike and his friends.

Growing Up

The sibling who spent the most time with young Mike was his older sister Jan. Because Mary Jo worked days and Leroy Sr. worked the night shift and slept during the day, Jan usually drove Mike to his Little League practices and games. It's a habit she found hard to break. Over the years, she probably has seen more of Mike's athletic events than any member of the family.

"I don't think I missed any of his college games," Jan says. "I haven't missed any of his Rams games."

The young Mike, she says, "kind of worried me at times. No girls. He was into his sports. He was not the ladies' man. He was shy. He married his first girlfriend—Misty."

School always came pretty easy. For example, Mike took high school math in grade school and college math in high school. He never got into much trouble, and when he did, it was almost always guilt by association. That is, his friends would get in trouble, and he just happened to be around.

"He did a few devilish things as he got older," Jan recalls. "He'd always call me to come and get him out of trouble. But it was normally because his friends put him up to it."

Like the time Mike, who was a high school senior, took the family car to visit Misty, his girlfriend. Jan was living on her own by then and got a call after 2 A.M. from Mike. He had wrecked the car, an old Chevy Impala, coming home. Or so he said.

Here's what really happened: He let a friend, James Garrett, borrow the car. The hours passed. Mike worried about Garrett's whereabouts. Finally around 2 A.M., he heard a car approaching. It sounded like a fender was dragging. Mike's heart sank.

"I'm thinking, 'Please, don't let it be my car,' " Mike says.

It was. James was returning the car but only after running into a tree. Trying to cover for James, Mike told Jan he had wrecked the car on the way home from Misty's house. That might have been the end of the story had Jan not inspected the accident scene. She wondered why the tree had been struck in the eastbound lane of the street. If Mike were on his way home, the accident would have been on the *westbound* side.

After this nifty piece of detective work by Jan, Mike 'fessed up and told her what really happened. "But I never told our parents," Jan says. (Maybe Leroy Sr. and Mary Jo won't read this page, or Mike might be grounded, retroactive to 1986.)

Mike wasn't always so magnanimous when it came to dealing with his friends. Kids can be brutally honest, and more than once young Mike went home crying after his friends had teased him about his ears. They called him *Spock.* Or *Dumbo ears.*

"I could take anything those guys could do except talk about me," Mike says. "They used to talk about my ears. And that used to drive me crazy. Because I have big ears. I can laugh at it now."

But not then. One day, Mike had had enough and fought one of his friends. No one teased him about his ears for years.

School Days

It didn't pay to tease Mike because he was always bigger than most and faster than most—which made for a potent combination in sports. Like all of his brothers and sisters before him,

Mike was sent to a Catholic high school—O'Hara. But he wasn't happy. It's not that he hated it at O'Hara, but all of his friends from the Paseo median were at Southwest High, a public school not far from the neighborhood. Mike asked his parents why he couldn't be with his friends.

"He accused me of a double standard because I was letting (younger sister) Kim go to Hogan," Mary Jo says. "Kim did not want to go to O'Hara. She wanted to follow her girlfriends to Hogan."

But Kim was merely switching from one Catholic school to another. Mike wanted to go from the Catholic system into the public school system. "Mom didn't want me to go to Southwest," Mike says.

But after one year at O'Hara, Mike got his way—at a cost. As a transfer student, he would be ineligible for varsity sports during his sophomore year.

Southwest High

From outside the building, Southwest High shows no signs of disrepair. The surrounding neighborhood appears vibrant, the housing reminiscent of the fashionable St. Louis Hills area of the Gateway City across the state. Former Kansas City Royals baseball great George Brett still lives near the high school. But one of the few signs that Southwest High School is closed is the bent goalpost crossbar on the football field—the field where Mike Jones matured into a young man and a NCAA Division I college prospect.

Southwest had a rich football tradition. Before Keith Hannaman took over in 1980, there had been only four head coaches in school history. "Everybody stayed there forever," Hannaman says. "Southwest High School was in the rich, white, Jewish, upper middle-class part of town. It had big community support."

But along with the desegregation of the Kansas City public school system came white flight. A lot of football talent migrated to Rockhurst, a private school and a state gridiron power.

Mike was always big for a running back, and to his surprise, he was put on the offensive line in his early practices with the Southwest Indians' junior varsity. Mike pleaded his case to the coach, so he appeared primed for a switch to running back, his natural position. Trouble was, the Southwest JV squad didn't have a quarterback. So the transfer from O'Hara went from running back to offensive lineman to quarterback. Mike opened the first JV game against Truman High of Independence, Missouri, at quarterback. But Mike the quarterback ran very well in that game—including a 55-yard scramble for a touchdown—opening everybody's eyes to his potential as a running back.

Hannaman, the Southwest varsity head coach, certainly took notice, realizing Mike would have been good enough to play varsity as a sophomore were it not for the transfer rule.

In the fall of 1985, Mike's junior season, he got his opportunity to play varsity football. Marvin Fight, one of Mike's good friends from the neighborhood, was a senior and the star of the Southwest backfield. He was also a major-college prospect. But in a preseason newspaper article, before Mike had played even one varsity game, Hannaman said: *"We have a great running back in Marvin Fight, but I think the person that's going to catch everybody's eyes is Michael Jones."*

It didn't look that way in the '85 season opener against Truman. Mike fumbled twice in his first varsity game. Everyone familiar with Southwest football knew what was coming next. All of the following week in school, Mike toted an old football Hannaman had filled with water. It was the coach's way of drilling into Mike's brain the importance of protecting the ball.

The next week against Lincoln Academy, a bunch of scouts were in the stands to watch

Fight. But Fight had injured his ankle in the opener the week before and didn't play. That meant Mike, wearing jersey number 44, got plenty of work in the backfield. Lincoln registered an upset victory but through no fault of Mike's. He rushed for 140 yards, which did not include a long run called back on a penalty. Although Mike was a junior, the college scouts who had come to watch Fight took notice.

For the third game of the season against Central, more scouts showed up to watch Fight. Again he was out of the lineup because of the ankle sprain. Southwest lost a classic mud ball tilt, but Mike sparkled once again. He topped 100 yards rushing for the second week in a row and would have topped 200 were it not for the fact that two long runs were nullified by penalties. And that rushing total would have been more like 250 yards were it not for one of life's most embarrassing moments.

"I pop a long run, and I'm going in to score," Mike recalls. "Most of the field's real muddy. I'm running on the muddy part of the field, so I'm trying to cut back to the dry part. I'm in the open field. I'm going for a touchdown because I'm starting to pull away from everybody. The fans are jumping up. And I just fall flat on my face. I could hear people laughing."

But the college scouts weren't laughing. The

next game, Fight returned to the lineup, which meant Mike got the ball less over the rest of the season. Southwest finished 4–6, its first losing season in years. Mike finished with a relatively modest 900 yards rushing. But thanks to those games against Lincoln and Central, he was now in the data banks of colleges throughout the Midwest and beyond.

Senior Success

Mike played fullback for Southwest and, at 6-feet 1-inch, 190 pounds, was a perfect fit for Hannaman's offense, which featured a lot of formations where the fullback was a lead blocker or ran quick hitters up the middle. Hannaman also liked to throw a play-action pass to the fullback.

"We ran that play forever and a day," Hannaman says. "So if Mike wasn't knocking someone down, he was pretending to knock someone down and then catching the ball."

Mike also was getting his share of carries. Southwest began the 1986 season with a bang, beating Truman for the first time in 12 years. It wasn't just the victory that was important, it was the way the Indians earned it. With Mike, wingback Paul Williams, and halfback Darroy Thornton each topping 100 yards, Southwest set a Missouri state record with 587 yards rushing.

Because of the monster rushing day, the Southwest team garnered a mention in *USA Today* and showed up on local television sports broadcasts. It looked like big things were on the way for Mike Jones and the Southwest Indians.

In fact, the Indians had a stellar season, and Mike rushed for more than 1,000 yards. As the victories piled up, more scouts began checking out Mike. There were several in the house when the Indians played arch rival Southeast High. Mike entered the game ranked among the state rushing leaders in Class 4A, but he ran into a stone wall against Southeast. He was held to five yards rushing. Southwest absorbed its only loss in what proved to be a 9–1 regular season.

After that game, some of the higher-profile schools recruiting Mike, including Notre Dame and Arizona State, quit calling. They had scratched him off their recruiting lists. Big Eight arch rivals Kansas and Missouri were shaping up as Mike's two biggest suitors. But wherever Mike ended up in college, the school was going to get a quality football player and a quality person, according to Hannaman.

"When you heard all the other kids talking about going out and getting drunk, getting stoned, or whatever over the weekend, Mike wasn't part of that," Hannaman recalls. "He was one of those kids who said, 'Yes, sir. No, sir.' He was up in front for every drill. If you were teaching something, Mike was there learning. He always helped out the other kids.

"He was a great peer mentor: *'Carry the ball this way. When we're running this play, take an extra half-yard split to the left. It's going to get you to the hole quicker.'* So what he learned from the coaches, he passed on to the kids."

Mike also proved to be quite the gentleman, as the entire Southwest High team discovered during the 1986 season when Stacy Simpson showed up on the practice field a couple weeks into the season. She was blonde, petite, and wanted to play football. She was given jersey number 47 and a spot on the JV squad at defensive back, officially making her the first female football player in the history of the Kansas City Interscholastic League.

One day, the junior varsity was working with the varsity during a tackling drill. "Mike comes up to carry the ball, and all the [junior varsity] defensive players kind of fade into the background," Hannaman remembers. "Nobody wanted to stand up against Mike."

At least none of the male players wanted the task. Suddenly, Stacy jumped out and yelled, *"I'll tackle him."*

This shaped up as a colossal mismatch. "Stacy was maybe 120 pounds," Mike remembers. "And I was like 190 pounds. She may have been 5-foot 2. I'm like 6-foot 1. I'm thinking, *'This just doesn't add up. If I'm running anything more than quarter-speed, I'm going to run right through her.'* "

Mike expressed those concerns to Coach Hannaman. *"Yeah, but she's got guts enough to stand in there against you. Go half-speed,"* Hannaman told Mike.

Mike did just that. He went half-speed and didn't put up much resistance. Down he went. Stacy Simpson had dropped the team's star running back in his tracks.

"She put her head in there and made the tackle," Hannaman recalls. "I never saw someone beam as much as this little girl did after the tackle."

Good for Stacy. But for Mike, the razzing was immediate and pointed from his teammates. *"You're soft, Mike. You're soft. You let a girl tackle you."*

A week or two later, Mike remembers that, "Stacy kind of disappeared." She was no longer on the team. Stacy Michelle Simpson had been arrested and charged with first-degree murder in the shooting death of her mother a year earlier. Eventually, she was sentenced to 11 years at the Chillicothe Correctional Center for voluntary manslaughter—the same town where Mike

Jones and the Southwest Indians would bring their state playoff dreams.

Playoff Bound

The Southwest varsity football team continued its stellar year, earning a postseason berth. The Indians opened the state playoffs at home against perennial state power Chillicothe. At least that was the plan.

"The kids were psyched," Hannaman says. "We were expecting 10,000 fans at the game." Then Hannaman got a call from the Missouri State High School Activities Association. According to an association official, because of the unseasonably cold mid-November weather, a water pipe had broken at the Interscholastic League stadium and made the field unplayable. The game was being moved to Chillicothe. This was all news to Hannaman, so he drove over to inspect the field.

"There's no broken water pipe," Hannaman recalls. "There's no water on the field. No ice. No nothing of any kind."

Southwest tried to fight the change of venue but was unsuccessful. Mike remembers driving by Interscholastic stadium on the way to Chillicothe. "The field looked fine," he remembers.

The field wasn't fine in Chillicothe, and neither was anything else. The field was frozen solid, devoid of grass. Chillicothe had plenty of heaters on its sidelines. There were none on the visiting sidelines, which were situated next to a parking lot full of excited Chillicothe fans.

"All the rednecks from Chillicothe were lined up in their pickup trucks, throwing beer cans at the kids," Hannaman says.

"It was a hostile crowd," Mike recalls.

To this day, Hannaman believes an official with the Missouri State High School Activities Association switched the game as a favor to a relative on the Chillicothe coaching staff.

"We got robbed," Hannaman says. "I felt so bad for the kids. The kids had worked so hard to have this home game their senior year, and then to have it just blown away. If we'd have played them at home, we would have won."

So Southwest lost to Chillicothe in the final game of Mike Jones' high school career

Choices

After the season, there was one important piece of gridiron-related business for Mike: choosing between the Kansas Jayhawks and the Missouri Tigers as the college of his choice.

Small-World Department: The main KU recruiter assigned to Mike was Jayhawks assistant coach George Warhop. In 1997, after signing a free-agent contract with the St. Louis Rams, Mike discovered that Warhop was an offensive line coach with his new team. It had taken 11 years, but Warhop finally got his man. (Warhop has since left the Rams for the Arizona Cardinals.)

Mike and his mother, Mary Jo, really liked George Warhop and KU head coach Bob Valesente. The campus was only 35 minutes from home. Warhop and Valesente told Mike he was their number 1 recruit and would be their featured tailback. Mike made a nonbinding verbal commitment to attend Kansas.

But Mizzou running backs coach Charles Coe wouldn't take no for an answer. He told Mike to ask Marvin Fight about Columbia, Missouri, and the Mizzou campus. Fight, Mike's former high school teammate, had made a recruiting trip a year earlier to Missouri, though he ultimately played junior college basketball elsewhere instead of college football.

Fight spoke so positively of his trip to Mizzou that Mike decided to make an official recruiting visit. The university sent a private jet to pick up Mike, Southwest High teammate Curtis Roberts, and three other area recruits.

Mike had a great weekend in Columbia. He hit it off with the other recruits and was impressed with Tigers head coach Woody Widenhofer. "He was a great salesman," Mike remembers.

It was still several weeks from signing day, but Mike knew then and there he wanted to attend Missouri. This meant the Tigers would double their recruiting pleasure because Mike and Roberts agreed at the end of the Southwest football season that they would attend the same college. The Jayhawks also were recruiting Roberts, a defensive end.

Little more than a week before signing day, the Southwest basketball team—which included Mike and Roberts—traveled to Columbia for a game with Hickman High. With both Coe and Warhop in attendance, it was time to tell Mizzou the good news—and Kansas the bad news.

But how? After a tough loss to Hickman, Mike and Curtis flipped a coin. Loser tells Kansas. Winner tells Mizzou. Mike called heads—and won. Thus Mike got to announce that he would become a Missouri Tiger.

Interestingly, no one recruited Mike at linebacker, the position he now plays in the National Football League. Not even Notre Dame and Arizona State, both of which had backed off early in the recruiting process, saw his potential at this position, despite the fact that in addition to running back, Mike had spent his entire high school career playing linebacker.

"I'll be honest with you, Mike was not a very good linebacker," Hannaman says. "He was just a good natural athlete that filled the position. He didn't stick his head in there. Now, if he was at running back going out to block a defensive end, he'd put his helmet right on the chest and knock the kid seven yards into the defensive backfield.

"But when he was at linebacker, and there was someone coming at him, he'd duck, he'd juke, he'd give him a shoulder. He didn't have the linebacker feel for the ball."

"My technique was terrible," Mike concedes. "All I did was, I'd see the ball, and I'd go run it down. That's pretty much all I did."

Which served him well against the lesser teams, but against well-disciplined squads that blocked well and ran traps and counters, Mike's linebacker play often suffered. Even so, Mike already displayed one attribute that served him well in Super Bowl XXXIV years later—"Mike was great on pass defense," Hannaman says. "Tremendous on pass defense."

Mizzou Blues

There was a time when losing football was neither expected nor tolerated at the University of Missouri. So one year after leading Mizzou to a Holiday Bowl game against Brigham Young University and quarterback Steve Young—yes, *that* Steve Young—coach Warren Powers was fired when the Tigers stumbled to a 3–7–1 record in 1984.

Powers' replacement, Woody Widenhofer, was hired with much fanfare. Widenhofer had been part of four Super Bowl championship teams as an assistant coach with the Pittsburgh Steelers. He was considered one of the architects of the famed "Steel Curtain" defense. Coach Woody didn't hesitate to flash one or more of his Super Bowl rings, which he wore with regularity. Mizzou faithful were invited to hitch a ride on Woody's Wagon by the school's marketing department.

But two years into the Widenhofer regime, Woody's Wagon had lurched into a ditch. After two seasons—and 22 games—Widenhofer had as many Super Bowl rings (four) as MU victories (four). Included in the loss column was Widenhofer's 1985 Mizzou debut, an ignominious defeat to then hapless Northwestern, and a 77–0 loss to Oklahoma—the worst defeat in school history—in a game dubbed the "Norman Conquest." (The game was played in Norman, Oklahoma, home of the Sooners.)

Woody's Wagon was broken, so Widenhofer set out to fix it, beginning with the recruiting class of 1987. Out went the pro-style offense. In came the "flexbone"—a version of the wishbone offense that featured three running backs in the backfield at the same time, an emphasis on ball control, the option, and power football.

A Cast of Thousands

Mike Jones was targeted as the number 1 backfield priority during the winter of 1986 by the Kansas Jayhawks. But after giving Kansas a nonbinding verbal commitment, Mike signed with Mizzou. He quickly discovered he was among a cast of thousands in the Tigers' backfield.

Mike was one of seven running backs Mizzou signed during that recruiting season. When he reported for his first preseason camp in August 1987, he was among 17 running backs on the Mizzou roster. One of them was second-year player Tony VanZant, perhaps the most heralded high school running back in the history of Missouri prep football. But VanZant was recovering from a serious knee injury.

To top it off, Curtis Roberts, Mike's friend and teammate from Southwest High, was academically ineligible after falling short of Proposition 48 requirements. So Mike was feeling a little low as he began preseason camp as the team's fifth-string fullback. He didn't want to get red-shirted as a freshman, but the situation didn't look promising.

That is, it didn't look promising until a pre-season scrimmage. "The first time I get the ball, we're running the option," Mike recalls. "I take it like 65, 70 yards for a touchdown." And this was against the first-team defense, no less.

"Everybody's looking at me like, *'Man, who is this?'*" Mike says. It was Michael Jones. (He went by Michael back then.) After that eye-opening performance in the scrimmage, he was elevated to second-team fullback behind starter Tommie Stowers. And that's where Mike stayed for his freshman season.

Stowers had a good year, so Mike didn't get to play a lot except on special teams. He did start two games because of an injury to Stowers, and he scored his only touchdown of the season against Oklahoma. His season totals: 22 carries for 99 yards.

Mike did seem to catch Widenhofer's eye on a Mizzou team that finished the 1987 season with a deceptive 5–6 record. "I just liked his demeanor and his personality," Widenhofer says. "He was a bright kid. Had a big smile all the time. Went to class. Practiced hard. Did everything you asked him to do. Of course, he was a pretty good student and had the athletic ability we needed to compete in that league."

Were it not for narrow defeats to Oklahoma, Oklahoma State, and Indiana that season, Missouri would have been bowl-bound, and Widenhofer would have been named Big Eight coach of the year. Besides Mike Jones, that Mizzou team included several players who not only made the pros, but started in the NFL: defensive back Erik McMillan, defensive end Jeff Cross, offensive tackle Carl Bax, running back Robert Delpino, and safety Harry Colon. McMillan made two Pro Bowls as a New York Jet, and Cross made one Pro Bowl appearance as a Miami Dolphin. Cross also was the Dolphins' season sack leader five times between 1989 and 1994.

Small-World Department: Robert Delpino led the *Los Angeles* Rams in rushing in 1991.

But Big Eight football, which has since expanded to the Big 12, was in its heyday. It seemed next to impossible to crack the upper division. Oklahoma State was in the midst of the Thurman Thomas/Barry Sanders era at running back. Colorado was beginning its rise to national prominence under head coach Bill McCartney. Led by the Bootlegger's Boy, Barry Switzer, Oklahoma led the league in victories, arrests, and colorful characters. And Nebraska was Nebraska, nearly unstoppable with a run-oriented offense as predictable as Tom Osborne's monotone.

If that weren't enough, Missouri played absolutely brutal non-conference schedules in those days. The Miami Hurricanes. Syracuse. Houston and its pinball machine offense of David Klingler and Andre Ware. Even Indiana, known as a basketball school, was in the midst of a gridiron renaissance under Bill Mallory. All told, five of MU's six losses in 1987 came against Top 20 teams. It was an early lesson to Mike that one solitary play could make the difference between winning and losing.

Switching Positions

Mike was ready to challenge Stowers for the starting fullback job in 1988, but he never got the chance. He was moved to halfback after the first spring scrimmage.

After rushing for 96 yards and two touchdowns in a season-opening victory over Utah State, Mike was stymied by a quicker-than-quick Houston defense—picking up only one yard on five carries.

Injury was added to insult in Game 3 when Mike suffered a broken hand in the first quarter against Indiana. But he kept playing. In fact, he scored the game-tying touchdown in the 28–28 tilt with the Hoosiers.

After missing the final non-conference game of the season at Miami, Mike returned for the conference opener against Kansas State wearing a bulky cast to protect his hand. Although his playing time was limited because of the injury, Mike earned the admiration of Widenhofer by racing 45 yards on an option pitch for the final TD in a 52–21 Missouri romp.

"If I had 11 Michael Joneses, we would be competing for the big ones right now—I guarantee you," Widenhofer told reporters after the game. *"He's a great kid. I think he's our best football player."*

Even with the injury, Mike finished the season as the team's second-leading rusher during his sophomore season with 463 yards on only 85 carries. But the efforts of Mike and the rest of the team couldn't save Widenhofer's job. Neither could a 55–14 thumping of rival Kansas in the 1988 finale. Mike rushed for 165 yards in that contest, a personal high at the college and high school levels.

"You could see the team getting better, but it was too late for Coach Woody," Mike says. "I thought he was a good coach. He was great to me."

The victory over KU meant Widenhofer had gone 3–1 against the Jayhawks in his four-year tenure. "And the next day I got fired," says Widenhofer, now head coach at Vanderbilt. "You used to get fired [at Mizzou] for *not* beating Kansas."

But the problem wasn't losing to Kansas. It was the fact that other than those three victories over the Jayhawks, Widenhofer had only nine triumphs in his other 40 games at Mizzou.

Coaching Changes and Diaper Changes

Enter Bob Stull, who had performed a minor miracle in resurrecting Texas-El Paso from the dregs of the Western Athletic Conference to a bowl game in 1988. By college standards, Stull ran a high-tech, pass-happy attack—a 180-degree change from the Widenhofer flexbone. Mike, a power back used to power football, would have to make a major adjustment to the new offense. But that wasn't the only adjustment Mike would make in his final two years of college.

Following his sophomore year at Mizzou, Mike married his high school sweetheart, Misty. She gave birth to their first daughter, Taelor, in September of Mike's junior season. Mike learned that Taelor was about to make her appearance one Monday morning when he stopped at the football office to return a VCR he had borrowed. There he learned that Misty had gone into labor. He rushed to Kansas City, where Misty had been staying with relatives, and arrived in time to see Taelor enter the world.

"He takes off Monday, misses practice," says Mike Ward, Mizzou's running backs coach under Bob Stull. "He calls me late Monday night, tells me about his baby girl, and tells me he'll be back for practice."

Mike was back on the practice field Tuesday. "That's Mike Jones right there," Ward says. His dedication to his family, and to his team, garnered him respect from the coaches and his teammates.

Meanwhile, football under Bob Stull featured more than its share of anxiety and ups and downs. As a junior, Mike surprisingly was beaten out for the starting tailback job by Jim White, a former non-scholarship walk-on from Independence Truman—the traditional opening-game opponent for Mike's high school team, the Southwest Indians.

"I thought it was my position to lose, and I thought I did enough to warrant that I would be the starting tailback," Mike says. "But when you have a new coaching staff coming in, sometimes they're going to make examples out of people. They've got to set a precedent, to let the players know that they're not going to accept losing and that you've got to do everything they want you to do. I think it was a thing where Jim played well and they just wanted to reward him."

White was a tough, savvy player who made the most of his ability—and a good guy to boot. It was easy to root for him. But in terms of pure athletic ability, there was no contest. Mike was clearly superior. The demotion was puzzling to Mike and his close friends. Mike was upset enough at the time that he told one of his best friends, Jimmy Collins, "I'm moving to defense. I'm going to take a redshirt year, and I'll play linebacker."

In fact, Mike began hitting the weight room like never before, trying to beef up in anticipation of a switch to linebacker. This took place *during* the 1989 season. "Me and JC [Collins] were hitting it," Mike recalls. "We were going like four days a week, lifting during the season."

Mike had entered the season weighing about 205 pounds, but he had bulked up to nearly 230 by season's end.

After a season-opening victory over Texas Christian, the Tigers offense got stuck in neutral in non-conference losses to Arizona State, Indiana, and Miami. During this time, the coaching staff switched Ronnell Kayhill to the halfback position, again to Mike's chagrin.

"That really got me upset because he hadn't played the whole season [at that position]," Mike says. "They had moved him to wide receiver."

Mike was reduced to mop-up duty in a Big Eight loss to Colorado, causing Buffaloes coach Bill McCartney to ask Tigers cornerback Adrian Jones: "What's up with Mike Jones? Why isn't he playing?" Adrian Jones didn't really have an answer. For his part, Mike Jones did no whining to his coaches.

"A lot of things that went on in '89, we really didn't know what the coaches wanted or what was going on," Collins remembers. "It was funny because they told Mike they were looking for more speed and quickness at the tailback position. Shoot, he was the fastest back we had."

True, Mike had superior straightaway speed, but he did lack the elusiveness and cutting ability of many elite tailbacks. He lacked "wiggle," as coaches like to say. As a result, it seemed the Stull coaching staff was always looking for somebody else to play at halfback during Mike's junior season.

"Mike didn't like it, but he was never going to complain," Collins says. "He was never the type of guy to say: 'The coaches don't like me.' You'd never get that from him."

Contributing to the inability to find the right role for Mike and others on the team was the problem of trying to fit flexbone running personnel into Stull's spread-the-field passing scheme. It was a classic case of trying to fit square pegs into round holes.

"We definitely had a bunch of that the first year," Ward recalls. "We played around, trying to do some I-formation, and realized we didn't have a real I-back. We had a fullback who didn't like to block in Tommie Stowers. Tommie was a great kid, but he wasn't a true blocking fullback."

And they had Mike and Jim White as their leading tailback candidates in a running game that required more reading of blocks and defenders than Mike had done under Widenhofer.

"Jim White did a nice job and outgraded Mike and outperformed him in certain situations," Ward says. "Mike was stiff and ran straight up. Not that Jim White was Gale Sayers, but he had a nice sense for some runs that we were doing."

Nonetheless, Mike began playing more as the season progressed, particularly around mid-season after White was sidelined by injury. Mike rushed for 133 yards against Kansas State, highlighted by a victory-clinching 67-yard TD run early in the fourth quarter of the 21–9 triumph. But that game marked only the Tigers' second victory of the season. It would be their last.

Stull's first Missouri team was crushed by another killer schedule. The Tigers were outscored 180–27 over a five-week stretch that saw them play the second-, third-, and fourth-ranked teams in the nation.

Even when the Tigers were competitive, things often went wrong. Against Oklahoma State, the Tigers scored a late TD to pull within 31–30 of the Cowboys, but Mike dropped a 2-point conversion pass from quarterback John Stollenwerck, and the Tigers lost.

In a wild season-ending loss to Kansas, Byron Chamberlain caught what appeared to be a game-tying 2-point conversion in the game's closing moments. But Chamberlain's feet landed barely out of bounds, and the Tigers lost 46–44.

Mike finished the season with only 343 yards rushing, down more than 100 yards from his 1988 total. On defense, the Tigers yielded a whopping 363 points, the most ever in the 99-year history of the program.

"It was ugly that year," Mike recalls. In Mike's mind, his NFL future looked so bleak at that point that he contemplated joining the Army after his college career ended.

Family Life and Football

By the time Mike began his senior season, Taelor was a regular at Mizzou's Dutton Brook-field practice facility. A diaper bag and a bottle were as much a part of Mike's daily equipment as his helmet and shoulder pads.

Depending on the time or circumstance, "Taelor would go to class with me. She would go to workouts at 6 A.M. with me. She'd watch film with me. She was part of the Breakfast Crew," Mike recalls. That's what the MU running backs dubbed themselves because of their early-morning get-togethers. It was nothing to see one of the running backs holding Taelor during a film session or Coach Ward baby-sitting while Mike ran a quick errand.

Between his teammates and friends, Mike says, "Taelor had a whole bunch of uncles and aunties up in Columbia."

One of those teammates, Jimmy Collins, a fullback who transferred to Mizzou from Illinois in 1988, is now a counselor and assistant football coach at Normandy High in suburban St. Louis. Collins remains one of Mike's best friends and is a regular volunteer at Mike's spring and summer football camps.

"He was a very dedicated father even then," Collins says. "He was able to juggle the responsibility of fatherhood and the demands of playing football." In a newspaper article at the time, Misty offered the following fatherhood report card on Mike:

- Changing diapers: A
- Late-night feedings: D
- Regular feedings: B-
- Discipline: D
- Playing with Taelor: A

Instead of eating at the team dining hall with the rest of the players, Mike requested—and received—an equivalent amount of money from the university added to his regular scholarship check.

"If he didn't eat in the dining hall, he could get more money on his scholarship check," Collins says.

Mike figured he could eat cheaply at home and use the extra money to help his growing family. A second daughter, Moriah, was born in

October 1990, during Mike's senior season. From time to time, his fellow running backs smuggled food out of the dining hall and over to Mike in the film room. Like Brenda Warner, wife of Rams quarterback Kurt Warner, Mike and Misty Jones were on food stamps for a while. Making ends meet wasn't easy.

"That was one of the things that was hard on Mike as his last few days at Missouri approached," Ward recalls. "He was trying to manage the family. We'd get him jobs when we could. Mike was always willing to do whatever he could to help his family at that point because he was in desperate situations at times."

Among Mike's part-time jobs in the spring and summer were jobs at a construction company and in a book warehouse. "We'd get him things for a week," Ward says. "There were people in Columbia that I'd call and say, 'I've got to get Mike Jones some money. He needs to work.' " And Mike would show up for work.

"The one thing Mike always felt in his heart was that he had to create a better life for himself and his family," Ward says. "It was family first. So I knew he was driven in many respects. I think that's an internal thing that has put him where he is today."

But Mike wasn't simply married with children. He was married with children at age 20 *and* playing Big Eight football *and* majoring in history. By the time his senior year rolled around, he became just as concerned with potty training as pass blocking.

The Tigers' head coach was sympathetic. *"Anybody that's ever had a kid, just to have that and go to work is tough,"* Stull said at the time. *"Here he is, he puts hours into football, and then he's got to go home and study. That's got to be extremely difficult. I think the players really respect him, look up to him, because he does handle things so well, and he is such a good competitor."*

In typical fashion, Mike shrugs off what must have been a stress-filled final two years at Mizzou. "It wasn't as hard as people think it was," Mike says. "Actually, my grades were better with my family in Columbia than when they weren't there."

A Season of Ups and Downs

Ward told Mike to get lighter and quicker for his senior season. From the end of November to mid-January, Mike worked out like a fiend. He lost about 25 pounds, returning to his previous playing weight of 205. Then, right before the start of spring football, the coaching staff switched gears again.

Instead of returning to halfback, Mike was told he would be the team's starting fullback for the 1990 season. It was a bittersweet promotion because Mike would start over his close friend—Collins. With Stowers now gone, Mike and Jimmy Collins had hoped to be Mizzou's starting backfield. Instead it was another year and another adjustment. The responsibilities of a fullback in Stull's offense were much different than under Widenhofer.

But with this latest switch, the Stull staff finally had figured out how best to use Mike. He ran more between the tackles, which was his strength. He proved to be a willing blocker. And Mike developed into a pass-receiving weapon as the season progressed. Stull's coaching staff may have vacillated in using Mike's skills, but they weren't slow in recognizing his character traits and leadership skills. Mike was named a team captain in 1990 along with Kent Kiefer, the starting quarterback.

"[Mike's] really consistent on a daily basis," Stull said at the time. *"The amazing thing is his work ethic. Every day he comes to work. Every day he does exactly what he's supposed to—to the best of his ability. On game day, it's the same thing."*

With Kiefer at quarterback, Mike at fullback, Tim Bruton at tight end, and Linzy Collins, Damon Mays, and Victor Bailey at wide receiver, the Tigers developed one of the nation's better passing offenses in 1990.

"We set up the run by passing," Mike says. "It's kind of similar to what we do here at the Rams." Such an arrangement meant Mike often got the ball 15 to 20 times a game. But sometimes, when the Tigers fell behind and had to play catch-up, he got it only five or six times.

"Our defense wasn't very good that year, but we could put some points on the board," Mike recalls. "We would go into meetings and our offensive coordinator (Dirk Koetter) would say, 'If they score 50, we've got to score 51.' I think that was the mentality of the whole coaching staff."

The approach, and the personnel, led to some wild fluctuations on the scoreboard. A late rally by TCU stunned the Tigers 20–19 in their season opener. Following a victory over Utah State, Mizzou was steamrolled 58–7 in Bloomington by Indiana.

Small-World Department: In his second college start, Hoosiers quarterback Trent Green completed seven of 11 passes for 154 yards and two TDs in Mizzou's loss to Indiana. Nine years later, Green signed a big free-agent contract with the Rams, only to have his 1999 season crash to an end with a preseason knee injury.

With 21st-ranked Arizona State in Columbia

the following week, Tigers fans braced for the worst. Surprise, surprise. With Mike scoring Mizzou's first touchdown on a 2-yard run, the Tigers spanked the Sun Devils 30–9. It was an emotional victory for Kiefer—the Mizzou quarterback who had once played for Arizona State. Ditto for Mays, the Mizzou wide receiver who was from Phoenix.

Small-World Department: During the game, Arizona State's highly regarded quarterback, Paul Justin, suffered a season-ending shoulder injury. Justin was signed as quarterback insurance for Warner in August 1999, following Trent Green's season-ending injury.

Even-Smaller-World Department: After the game, Arizona State assistant coach Mike Martz stopped by the Mizzou locker room to say hello to Kiefer and Mays. Martz, of course, masterminded the Rams' take-no-prisoners attack as offensive coordinator on the Super Bowl squad, then succeeded Dick Vermeil as head coach.

After the Arizona State game, the Tigers were 2–2, and all things seemed possible. With 12th-ranked Colorado coming to town for the Tigers' Big Eight opener, there was an air of anticipation that hadn't been felt in Columbia for years. What transpired was one of the most memorable games in college football history—the infamous Fifth-Down Game.

The Tigers couldn't stop Colorado's potent option offense. But the Buffaloes couldn't stop Kiefer and Mays. Keifer threw for 326 yards and three TDs. Mays caught five balls for 153 yards and two TDs. The last of those catches, a 38-yard TD reception with 2:32 to play, gave Mizzou a 31–27 lead and seemingly clinched a dramatic upset over the defending Big Eight champions.

Colorado took over on its 12 on the ensuing kickoff—88 long yards away from a touchdown. But the Buffaloes gobbled up most of those yards with surprising speed for a running team. With one timeout remaining and 31 seconds to play, the Buffaloes were first-and-goal on the Mizzou 3-yard line. Then, here's what happened:

- **First down:** CU quarterback Charles Johnson intentionally spiked the ball, stopping the clock with 28 seconds to play.

- **Second down:** CU tailback Eric Bieniemy ran up the middle for two yards. The Buffaloes used their last timeout with 18 seconds to play.

- **Third down:** Bieniemy tried the middle of the

line again, only to be stopped for no gain. Under most circumstances, the Buffaloes wouldn't have had time to run another play before time expired. But officials ruled the Tigers were late getting off the pile and stopped the clock with 8 seconds to play.

- **Fourth down:** With the sideline marker showing it was only third down, and the clock now running, Johnson spiked the ball again to stop the clock with 2 seconds remaining. (The chain gang had failed to flip the down marker from second to third down after Bieniemy's first run.)

- **Fifth down:** On a quarterback keeper to his right, Johnson scored on a 1-yard run as time expired.

The scene after the game was surreal. Thinking Johnson had been stopped short of the goal line, hundreds of Mizzou fans stormed the field, tearing down the goalposts in glee. Other fans, who saw the officials signal touchdown—and who also knew how to count to five—stormed the field and angrily chased the officiating crew off the field. Mizzou players went to their locker room, took off their shoulder pads, and came back onto the field while officials huddled and tried to sort out the mess.

"The thing about it, people on the sidelines

knew that it was five downs," Jimmy Collins recalls. "They were saying, 'Hey, coach! That's five downs!' People knew before the play even went off that it was five downs."

Well, some people on the MU sidelines knew this but apparently not everyone. "We were so caught up in that moment," Mike remembers. "It was just a situation where the coaches, the players, the officials, the fans—unless you were a person that was ultra-calm—you would have gotten caught up in the moment."

As the Tigers milled around in the locker room after the game, word quickly spread from player to player: *That was fifth down. It was fifth down.* About 20 minutes after the game ended, the officials' debate ended. The game was declared over. Final score: Colorado 33, Missouri 31.

That night, Heidi's Deli in Columbia served a drink called the Fifth Down. Exact ingredients were unknown, but proprietors said it was one more than the rules allowed. Mike Jones and Jimmy Collins stayed up late that night, talking about the game.

"Maybe they're going to reverse the decision," Jones remembers telling Collins.

But that was not to be. In 1940, Cornell scored the game-winning touchdown on the fifth down in a 7–3 Ivy League victory over Dartmouth. The decision was later reversed and Dartmouth was awarded a 3–0 victory. Since that Cornell-Dartmouth game, rule changes in college football made it technically impossible to correct such an error.

"The rule says any decision that is changed has to be made before the ball is next put in play," David Nelson, secretary editor of NCAA football rules, explained the day after the Mizzou-Colorado game. *"Once they snapped the ball for the next down, which was the fifth down, then they couldn't change it."*

Besides, Nelson said MU coaches, *"should have known what down it was."* To which Bob Stull replied, *"A lot of people did. Several of our coaches tried to yell at the officials. Fans tried to yell at them. But they wouldn't acknowledge us, which they should do."*

But several Missouri players, and apparently coaches, too, thought Stull should have done more. "He should have run out onto the field [to protest] and got a flag," Collins says. (With the ball on the one-yard line before Johnson's fifth-down run, even a penalty would have advanced the ball only to the half-yard line.)

"But if you remember, Coach Stull was so conservative," Collins says. "I can always remember this: The coaches were very upset with Coach Stull. It was a very long week. There was a lot of anxiety. I think the most shocking thing about that whole weekend is what Coach Stull said the next day in team meetings. He said, 'Well, if we would have stopped them on fifth down, we would have still won the game.'

"I think it kind of crushed the kids on the defensive side of the ball. Give the guys some credit. We just beat the 12th-ranked team in the country. The defense is already struggling. The guys were very surprised at Coach Stull's response. I guess that was [supposed to be] a way to motivate us. We were going into Nebraska the next week. But if you remember, we went up to Nebraska and got our [butts] kicked."

Although not as vocal on the topic, Mike agrees with Collins' basic assessment. "I thought, personally, that Coach Stull could have done more," Mike says. "He could have said more. It was like, 'We lost. We lost.' I just thought something else could have been done."

That Monday, the Big Eight indefinitely suspended the seven-member officiating crew—headed by referee J.C. Louderback. The Buffaloes went on to share the national title with Georgia Tech. But here's the kicker: It looked like Colorado quarterback Charles Johnson didn't even get into the end zone on fifth down. Although this wasn't a nationally televised game with a multitude of camera angles to choose from, game film, and a series of photos in a Columbia newspaper, seemed to indicate that Johnson didn't make it into the end zone.

"His head was on the goal line, but the ball never crossed the plain," Collins says. "He was on his back, then he reaches the ball over the plain."

The thought of Johnson lunging desperately toward the goal line on the final play of the game sounds eerily similar to what happened in Super Bowl XXXIV a decade later. Tennessee Titans receiver Kevin Dyson lunged desperately toward the goal line on the final play of the game but was stopped short of a touchdown by Mike Jones.

People often ask Mike where he was on the final play of the Fifth-Down Game. Did he come close to tackling Charles Johnson? Actually he was nowhere near the play. Mike was a *running back* in college—not a *linebacker*. Mike had rushed for 49 yards and a touchdown on seven carries and caught five passes for 49 yards against Colorado. A decent game, to be sure, but instead of being in position to make a victory-saving tackle, Mike was watching the final play from about the 25-yard line.

Gains and Losses

Sports fans sometimes forget that between games, athletes face the same trials and tribulations of everyday life as "civilians." Mike was no different. Complications in her pregnancy caused Mike's wife, Misty, to be hospitalized before the Fifth-Down Game. On October 11, 1990—five days after the Colorado game and two days before facing Nebraska—Misty gave birth to their second daughter, Moriah. A little more than one week later, or one day before playing Kansas State, Mike got a phone call telling him that Misty had been involved in an accident while going to visit Moriah at the hospital. (Moriah had an extended stay in the hospital because she was born two months premature.) Misty had a minor neck injury but was fine otherwise.

"It didn't seem real tough, to be honest with you," Mike says. "It was like something happened, and you've got to deal with it."

If only the Mizzou football team could have taken the same approach in the aftermath of the Fifth-Down Game. The "defeat" seemed to drain the life from the team and suck the air out of a once-promising season.

The Tigers were hammered 69–21 the following week by seventh-ranked and unbeaten Nebraska. Mike carried only seven times for

21 yards against the Cornhuskers but flashed his developing receiving skills with six catches for 118 yards and two TDs. He had 111 yards rushing and receiving the following week in a 31–10 triumph over Kansas State, catching a 23-yard TD pass for MU's first score. Next came a 130-yard rushing performance and two TDs in Stillwater in a 48–28 loss to Oklahoma State.

Mike twisted his ankle late in the third quarter against Oklahoma State, limiting his effectiveness late in the game. The combination of a gimpy ankle and a 3–5 record gave the Mizzou coaching staff an excuse to start looking toward the 1991 season. Beginning with the Oklahoma game the following week, and continuing with the Iowa State contest and the season finale against Kansas, freshman fullback Michael Washington began getting more playing time—at Mike's expense.

"I thought that was wrong because after the Oklahoma State game, I was leading the Big Eight in catches," Mike recalls. "I guess I was about sixth in rushing, and I was like maybe second in touchdowns scored. So I was having a really good year."

The lack of playing time made for a bittersweet ending to Mike's college career. "The only thing that helped was we beat Kansas that last game of the season, and we beat them in Kansas," Mike says.

The End and the Beginning

Like former coach Woody Widenhofer, Mike Jones left Mizzou with a 3–1 record against the Jayhawks. By this time, Bob Valesente no longer was Kansas head coach. George Warhop, the KU assistant who had doggedly recruited Mike out of high school, was at Vanderbilt. And of those seven running backs Widenhofer recruited to Mizzou in 1987, only two—Mike and Sean Moore—were still on the Mizzou roster.

The Tigers ended their 100th season of varsity football with a 4–7 record. Mike led the Tigers in rushing with 485 yards and caught 41 passes—a school record for a running back. It had been a solid, but not spectacular, college career.

"We've been through so many things. I can actually say I've been through everything," Mike said at the time. "We let a lot of games just slip out of our hands."

Who knows what would have happened to the Missouri program—and to Mike's career— had the Tigers been awarded a victory over Colorado. It might have gotten Mizzou over the hump and gotten Mike more exposure as a running back.

"A lot of guys carried the Fifth-Down game with them after their careers at Missouri were gone," Collins says. "The year that Mizzou finally beat Colorado [1997], I talked to Mike for a couple of hours. Because it was kind of like that win was our win."

But in the weeks and months immediately after the 1990 season, Mike Jones didn't look back. He only looked forward—to the NFL draft.

5

You Are Now a Linebacker

Having a good college career isn't enough to ensure a job in the National Football League, and it hasn't been for quite some time. Before investing hundreds of thousands of dollars in a player—in many cases millions of dollars—NFL teams want to know more about a prospect than can be learned from college game film.

Player evaluation has become a science, albeit an inexact science. Every NFL team has an extensive college scouting department, made up of men—and in a few cases, women—whose sole job is to judge college talent.

As a result, the four months between the end of the college season and the NFL draft in April is a critical time for prospective NFL rookies. A player's draft outlook can rise or fall dramatically without completing a pass, running for a first down, or making a tackle.

Draft Preparation

Mike was invited to play in the Blue-Gray all-star game in Montgomery, Alabama, a good first step in the predraft process. Scouts, coaches, and personnel officials use these contests to watch the best draft prospects in the country work against one another, so even the workouts leading up to the actual all-star game are important.

After a good week of practice, Mike strained a hamstring the day of the game—actually while he was stretching before the game, of all things. Although not a serious injury, his effectiveness was limited in the contest. More important, the hamstring problem hampered Mike's ability to train for the NFL Scouting Combine in Indianapolis a month later. After taking a couple weeks off to let the hamstring heal, Mike wasn't at full speed for this huge job fair for NFL prospects. (Each year at the Scouting Combine, about 300 prospects are timed and tested by scouts; poked and prodded by doctors; and interviewed and questioned by coaches over a three-day period.)

Mike did well in many of the drills, particularly the vertical jump and the broad jump. But his hamstring injury caused him to run a slow time—at least by his usual standards—in the all-important 40-yard dash.

"I think I ran about a 4.65," Mike says. "It was the slowest time I'd run in a long time." In college, he had consistently run in the 4.5-second range, occasionally dipping down to 4.4 seconds, which is very fast for a 215-pound running back.

Draft Anticipation

In 1991, the draft lasted 12 rounds over two days; it has since been trimmed to only seven rounds. Mike and his agent, Harold Lewis of St. Louis, were hopeful that some NFL team would call Mike's name in the middle rounds—somewhere between rounds four and eight.

"People really liked him, but he didn't have the big, giant size as a fullback," Lewis says. By NFL standards, Mike was a classic 'tweener: not big enough to play fullback and not elusive enough to play halfback. But Mike scored high when it came to intangibles.

"He was successful in everything he did," Lewis says. "He was the leader on the field and the leader off the field, just like he is today. On every play he gave 100 percent when you looked at the tape on him."

Mike approached the draft with a realistic sense about his NFL future. But those who knew him well realized he was under pressure from several sources. "He was starting to have some hard times with his wife at that time, and that was really weighing on him," says Mike Ward, Mike's position coach at Mizzou. "So he was going through some tough times at the end of his [college] eligibility and moving into the draft period."

Draft Disappointment

On April 21, the first day of the draft, Mike's brother Kevin threw a party at his house. Only three rounds were to be selected on Day 1. Because Mike knew he wouldn't be drafted that early, everyone expected to enjoy the party without any anxiety or nervousness.

But Kansas City selected Louisiana State running back Harvey Williams with the 21st selection in the first round. Then the New York Giants took Michigan running back Jarrod Bunch with the 27th overall pick in the round. And midway through the second round, San Francisco drafted Notre Dame running back Ricky Watters. This wasn't a good development. The Chiefs, Giants, and 49ers were all teams that had shown interest in Mike before the draft.

"I'm scrambling now," Mike recalls.

Things got worse the next day, April 22. Much worse. Mike figured he'd go early on Day 2. At this time, there was no televised coverage of the second day of the draft, so Mike could only sit by the phone and wait.

"By 10:30 A.M., I'm already going crazy," Mike says. "I'm thinking, *'What's going on?'* "

Early in the fifth round, Denver selected University of Washington running back Greg Lewis. The Broncos also had seemed very interested in Mike.

At the end of the eighth round, Mike's agent called. He had nothing specific to tell Mike, just words of encouragement: *"Hang loose. Something will happen."* At the end of the ninth round, the Cleveland Browns called, telling Mike they were thinking of taking him in the 10th round. The round came and went, but nothing happened.

"I'm basically pacing back and forth," Mike recalls.

Harold Lewis called again after Round 10. *"The Raiders are thinking about taking you,"* Lewis told Mike. But Mike couldn't take it anymore. He left the house with a friend, Arthur Armstrong, and headed to Arleta Park, where Mike frequently trained. He began running hills to work off the pent-up energy of the day.

Round 12 came and went. The draft was over, and Mike's name hadn't been called. To say he was feeling low would be an understatement. "What would you feel like if someone told you that you'd be better off doing something else?"

Mike says. At that point, that's what Mike felt the entire National Football League was telling him.

That same night, the Raiders called to say they wanted to sign Mike as an undrafted free agent. They wanted him to play—linebacker!

Linebacker?

"You've got the wrong Mike Jones," Mike remembers telling the Raiders. He was being serious, not sarcastic. Mike thought the Raiders had him confused with Mike Jones the defensive end from North Carolina State.

Small-World Department: Little did either Mike Jones know at the time, but they would end up as Rams teammates seven years later for the 1998 season.

What Mike Didn't Know

No, the Raiders had the right Mike Jones. But what made them think he could play linebacker in the NFL? Actually the topic had come up on more than one occasion during Mike's college career at Mizzou.

"There were battles to move him to defense all the time," recalls Woody Widenhofer, Mike's head coach at Missouri in 1987 and 1988. Maybe so, but none of this made its way back to Mike. Looking back, Mike does remember some peculiar comments made by assistant coach Charles Coe.

Coe, remember, had recruited Mike out of high school and was the running backs coach during Mike's freshman year of college. But Coe was reassigned to defense in 1988, and after making the switch, he'd frequently tell Mike: *"I'm going to get you over here."*

"I thought he was just playing," Mike says. But maybe he wasn't. The point became moot after Widenhofer's dismissal, but the new staff headed by Bob Stull had similar discussions.

"Everything we talked about had to do with personnel," Ward says. "Where can we get people to help the team win?"

Ward and defensive coordinator Mike Church talked about linebacker play a lot. "There were times where I would say to Church, 'Mike Jones would be a great weakside linebacker for you,' " Ward says. "Church would say, 'Are you kidding me? I'll take him right now.' "

Church also suggested that another Mizzou running back from the Widenhofer era, Tommie Stowers, would make an outstanding strongside linebacker. (Strongside linebackers play over the tight end; weakside linebackers play more in space—or in open areas.)

"My position was, 'Well, you can't get them both in our first year,' " Ward recalls.

If a switch was to be made, Mike seemed a

more logical linebacker choice than Stowers because Mike had two years of eligibility remaining. Stowers had only one. By the time Stowers learned the linebacker position, his college career would be over.

Ward actually brought the suggested switch to a staff meeting that spring—before Mike had played a game for Stull. The notion was shot down—quickly.

"No way! We can't do that. We can't do that. We've got to have Mike Jones at running back," was the sentiment expressed by other coaches in the room. "And they're looking at me like I'm an idiot," Ward remembers. "Here I am the running backs coach, and I'm going to give up one of my best guys."

The subject pretty much died right there, even though Mike—upset over his temporary demotion to second-team halfback behind Jim White—spent much of his junior season bulking up in the weight room to make a switch to linebacker in 1990.

It's a switch that never happened. After signing linebacker recruits Darryl Major and Travis McDonald, the Tigers figured they'd be better at the position in 1990 even without Mike.

But Ward never abandoned the concept—not in his head, at least. "Mike just did things athletically that limited him on the next level as a running back but opened the door for him as a linebacker," Ward says. "He wasn't going to play in the NFL as a fullback. He wasn't big enough. And he certainly wasn't going to play at tailback because he didn't have the wiggle. So he was caught."

Checking Out Mike

Little did Ward know at the time, but he and the Raiders were working in a parallel universe—both were thinking about Mike Jones as a linebacker.

Sometime during the 1990–91 school year—Mike's senior year at Mizzou—a Raiders official paid a visit to Keith Hannaman, Mike's high school coach in Kansas City. "The Raiders' undercover man, I like to call him," Hannaman says. "He was a retired FBI agent who did all the character checks for the team. Very, very nice gentleman. Gray hair, mid 60s. I can't remember his name."

(During the course of an interview for this book, Raiders owner Al Davis declined to comment on this "undercover man" or his activities. So we'll call him Mr. X and point out that it is routine for NFL teams to do background checks on players. It's another facet of the evaluation process.)

During his trip to Kansas City, Mr. X talked to Mike's minister, his teachers, and of course, Hannaman. "I told him, no drugs, no alcohol," Hannaman says. "He treats his girlfriend nice. Great family support. Says, 'Yes, sir. No, sir.'" (At the time, Hannaman couldn't help chuckling to himself. Mike's rock-solid background didn't exactly square with the Raiders' rough-and-tumble image.)

Then the conversation took an unexpected turn.

Mr. X: "We're going to make him a linebacker."

Hannaman: "What?"

Mr. X: "Oh yeah, we think we can convert him into one heck of a linebacker."

Hannaman: "You guys have seen all of his film, haven't you? If you look at his high school film at linebacker, you might change your mind."

Mr. X: "Oh no. He's a heck of an athlete. We think we can make a linebacker out of him."

Remember, Hannaman didn't think Mike was much of a linebacker at Southwest High. Hannaman may have had his doubts about Mike as an NFL linebacker prospect, but Mike Ward didn't.

"Mike was being told, 'You're going to be drafted here. You're going to be drafted there.

Don't worry. You're going to be a fullback,' "
Ward says. "Nobody else was looking at this guy
as a linebacker. Nobody was even thinking about
that."

Well, the Raiders were—Ward just didn't
know it at the time. So when the Raiders sent
him a player evaluation form on Mike to be filled
out well before the draft, Ward went beyond the
expected.

"It was a one-page deal," Ward says. "I
ended up doing three pages. I did a whole dis-
sertation on Mike, went through everything on
him. And I sent it right to Al Davis."

In the report, Ward suggested strongly that
Mike's future in the NFL was at linebacker, not
running back. "I just wrote about his abilities
and how they would apply to the linebacker position," Ward says. "His athleticism. His character. His intelligence.

"I knew Mike would grasp what was happening at linebacker, would take the time to
learn. The physical part of the game on
defense—he would have no problem with that.
He would get bigger. He would get stronger. The
Raiders knew that, they saw that, they engaged
in it."

Ward sent this Mike-as-linebacker information only to the Raiders. He knew the organization as a whole, and Al Davis in particular, as a

group of free thinkers when it came to personnel. As Ward puts it, "They liked to think outside the box."

In other words, the Raiders routinely looked for projects, scouring the smaller colleges for unknown or unheralded prospects. Occasionally, they drafted college players at one position with the idea of switching them to another. And they were always on the lookout for speed.

Al and Mike

Nearly a decade after the fact, Al Davis has vague recollections of that Mike Ward report. "I do remember something like that—that someone brought up the fact that Mike Jones might have those qualities to play linebacker," Davis says. "I was thinking of it before I read the report. But that more or less authenticated and helped my belief."

Davis first seriously thought about Mike as a linebacker after watching him work out at the NFL Scouting Combine. Mike may not have been pleased with his 40-yard dash time, but Davis thought he ran well.

"I watched him in his movement," Davis says. "I thought he would make an excellent third-down linebacker who could cover backs, who could run well. But he would have to work at it.

"We couldn't draft him as a running back because down deep we didn't believe he was a running back. He had running skills, but to be one of your top running backs, you have to have certain abilities that I just didn't think he had. But as soon as the draft was over, he was one guy that we pinpointed, that we wanted right away. Our people had met with him."

Referring to those meetings, Davis says, "I wanted to know: Was the passion there? Was the intensity? Would he work? That was the key. Because a lot of times when you are moving people to other positions, they have to have that commitment and passion. He had played linebacker as a high school player, so I knew that wouldn't be foreign to him."

Davis says every team in the NFL at that time was looking for linebackers who could play man-to-man pass coverage on running backs. Davis thought Mike could develop those skills, given time and patience. Besides, Mike reminded him of former Raiders linebacker Rod Martin, who once set a Super Bowl record with three interceptions.

Small-World Department: Rod Martin's three INTs came in Super Bowl XV—in 1981—at the expense of the Philadelphia Eagles and a young firebrand coach named Dick Vermeil.

Nineteen years later, the player who reminded Davis so much of Martin—Mike Jones— would help Vermeil and the Rams defeat Tennessee in Super Bowl XXXIV.

Al Davis has a long track record of success with position switches. He turned Ethan Horton into an All-Pro tight end from a college running back. Matt Millen played defensive line for Penn State but became an accomplished linebacker for the Raiders. Famed Raiders cornerbacks Lester Hayes and Willie Brown played different positions in college.

Perhaps Davis' greatest success at position switches had occurred in the late 1960s, when Davis switched 6-foot, 5-inch Gene Upshaw, an offensive tackle from tiny Texas A&I, to offensive guard.

"Everyone said, 'He's crazy. There's no guard in the world who could be 6-foot, 5,'" Davis recalls. (Conventional wisdom at the time held that short, quick guards were best.) "But I had to stop Buck Buchanan with the Chiefs. He was an animal. I had to get someone as big as him and as good as him."

Buchanan became a Hall of Fame defensive tackle for Kansas City. And Upshaw? Now executive director of the NFL Players Association, Upshaw became the premier guard of his era. He played in three Super Bowls, made seven Pro Bowls, and was elected into the Pro Football Hall of Fame in 1987.

But all of those success stories had one thing in common: Davis had moved players to new positions *on the same side of the ball.* In Mike's case, the Raiders were trying to switch a player from offense (running back) to defense (linebacker). That just doesn't happen very often in today's NFL.

"Look at all the rosters in the NFL," Ward says. "Call me back and tell me if you can find more than three [similar changes]."

Raider Bound

Back to the draft. Or, in Mike's case, the non-draft. By the 11th or 12th round, Mike's agent, Harold Lewis, knew it would be better if his client weren't drafted. (After the draft, teams frequently sign several rookie free agents to minimum-wage contracts. These rookies are a source of cheap labor and help fill out rosters for training camp. A very low percentage of these players actually make NFL teams, but in the hours immediately following the draft, the competition can be heated to sign them.) According to Lewis, Mike had plenty of options from which to choose immediately after the draft ended.

"This is a true story, I'm telling you straight up," Lewis says. "Mike got phone calls from at least 17 teams interested in him as an undrafted free agent. They all wanted him as a fullback, except one team. The Raiders.

"I get a call from Bruce Kebric, who's still with the Raiders in player personnel. He tells me that Al Davis loves Michael Jones as a linebacker and that he believes that's his natural position. To be honest, I was hesitant about it."

Ward recalls that Lewis was more than "hesitant" about sending Mike to the then-Los Angeles Raiders to play linebacker.

"I get a hold of Mike after the draft," Ward says. "He says, 'My agent's got me going to Denver as a fullback.' I said, 'You're going to L.A. tomorrow, and you're trying out as a linebacker, and you're going to sign with the Raiders.' "

Meanwhile Kebric and the Raiders were giving Lewis the hard sell.

Lewis: "Bruce, I think the world of you, but this guy's a running back."

Kebric: "Harold, I'm telling you, when Al puts his mind to something and Al likes somebody, you've got nothing to worry about."

Lewis remained skeptical, until he got a call from Davis. *"I'm guaranteeing you that Mike is going to be one of my guys, and he's going to be here,"* Davis told Lewis.

"Now, who else is going to make you that kind of guarantee?" Lewis says with a laugh.

Landing a Job

So on April 22, only hours after the draft ended, Mike headed for Los Angeles and a workout with the Raiders' staff. If the workout didn't go well and the Raiders' withdrew the offer, he could always sign with one of the other teams who remained interested in him as a fullback. It never got to that point.

Small-World Department: His first morning in L.A., Mike had breakfast with Raiders' personnel official Steve Ortmayer. In 1995, Ortmayer joined the Rams as vice president of football operations, just in time for the move to St. Louis. After two seasons in St. Louis, Ortmayer was fired. Because of one of his failed personnel moves—the signing of free-agent linebacker Carlos Jenkins in 1995—the Rams looked for a new outside linebacker in 1997. They signed Mike Jones to replace Jenkins.

At that 1991 breakfast in Los Angeles, Steve Ortmayer welcomed Mike to the Raiders and reiterated the team's intentions to try him at linebacker. Curious, Mike asked why. Ortmayer said Mike Ward had told the Raiders that Mike might be a decent NFL running back, but he could be a great NFL linebacker.

At the time, Mike was miffed to hear this explanation. "I'm out here trying to make it as a running back in the NFL and my running back coach tells them I'm a better linebacker," Mike recalls. "If I'm an NFL scout, I'm thinking, *'This guy can't play running back.'* "

At his workout that day, Mike ran a very good 40 time. Two Raiders defensive backs, Terry McDaniel and Lionel Washington, were so impressed they asked him what position he played. "Fullback," Mike remembers telling them.

McDaniel and Washington ran back into the locker room and came back with starting fullback Steve Smith. They all watched the rookie run. But when it was time for some drills, Mike performed for Raiders *linebacker* coach Gunther Cunningham—now head coach of the Kansas City Chiefs.

Cunningham had Mike do pass-drop drills, change-of-direction drills, and drills in which he had to read run or pass. The pass drops seemed to come easy. Reading plays was another thing. "At the time, I was totally clueless," Mike admits.

The workout went well, and Mike signed his

first NFL contract. Al Davis and the Raiders made it very clear financially that they believed Mike had potential. Most undrafted free agents get only a few thousand dollars in guaranteed signing bonus money. Mike received a two-year deal that included a $15,000 signing bonus, a $5,000 reporting bonus (for showing up on time for training camp), a preseason bonus of $2,500, relocation bonuses totaling $25,000, and a roster bonus of $25,000 (for making the final roster at the start of the 1991 regular season).

All told, it was a contract equivalent to what a sixth- or seventh-round pick might have received at the time. "For a college kid who wasn't making any money, to be making $2,000 or $3,000 a week, you could live with that," Mike says.

Meanwhile, Mike Ward had asked the Raiders for one thing if Mike made it to Los Angeles: a videotape of his first workout with the Raiders. Ward wanted to see what the Raiders did with Mike and how Mike performed.

"I think I got a tape delivered overnight," Ward says. "And it shows exactly what he did. All the workouts. Coverage drills." Ward was impressed with what he saw. "Nice and fluid. Boy, he was smooth."

The tape gave Ward some peace of mind. His job was done in terms of getting an NFL team to look at Mike at linebacker. But he has continued to follow Mike's career from afar with great satisfaction.

"I daresay there were a ton of linebackers drafted that year that aren't in the league, and he still is," Ward says. "He got better, he got better, he got better. He signed a big seven-digit contract. And now he's Mr. Tackle."

Early Challenges

When Mike arrived in Los Angeles for his first Raiders minicamp later in the spring of 1991, he figured he'd quickly be Mr. Unemployed. Mike reported at 220 pounds, but immediately felt like the guy who gets sand kicked in his face by the beach bully. The competition at linebacker literally looked formidable.

"I had heard about Winston Moss, but I didn't know how big he was," Mike says. "Winston came into minicamp and he was probably 270 pounds. We had like five or six guys that were 250 pounds-plus playing linebacker. I mean, these guys are enormous. That first day, I'm thinking, *'I'm not going to make it. I am too small. I've got to gain the weight and quick.'*"

Then the drills started.

During one drill, the offensive guard pulls— or runs quickly down the line of scrimmage to block. The outside linebacker is supposed to challenge the guard, knock him off his course, and disrupt the play. When it was Mike's turn at outside linebacker, massive Raiders guard Todd Peat heads toward the line of scrimmage.

Now Peat is a walking fire hydrant, conservatively listed at 315 pounds. In truth, he outweighed Mike by more than 100 pounds.

"That's the first person I run into, or try to run into," Mike says. It's a one-sided collision.

"Peat just sends me rolling," Mike admits. "It was comical that first day."

After a practice full of misadventures, Mike is advised by his coaches to slow down and try to react to what he sees, instead of just flying toward the ballcarrier or blocker.

By the end of that first minicamp, Mike began to show improvement. The Raiders sent Mike back to Columbia with a set of equipment—shoulder pads, other pads, helmets, etc. They wanted him to work on drills wearing full pads back home. They also gave him tapes to watch.

But in Mike's mind, no matter how hard he worked, the numbers game didn't look promising. In addition to perhaps 10 returning players, the Raiders had drafted two linebackers, and Mike was among three undrafted linebackers signed by the club that spring. Mike knew that when the final roster was set, the Raiders would keep only six or seven. Mike was showing rapid improvement, but he was so raw at the position, sometimes he felt as though he didn't belong at subsequent minicamps.

"I know there were people thinking, 'Man, who is this guy?'" Mike says.

Preseason Lessons

Despite the fact that Raiders owner Al Davis had taken an interest in Mike, the two men didn't meet until Mike's first NFL training camp, which took place nearly three months after the draft.

"Al pulled me aside and said they would give me a chance to learn the position," Mike recalls. "He said, 'Mike, just learn what you have to do. You've got some ability.' He was real patient with me. Al's always been good to me."

It seemed Davis' early confidence in Mike was paying off. By the time training camp started, Mike had moved up to third team on the depth chart, but he'd have to make the second team to have a realistic chance to make the squad.

In the Raiders' 1991 preseason opener against San Francisco, Mike learned the difference between practice speed and game speed— the hard way. Playing special teams for the first time since his freshman year at Mizzou, Mike sprinted down the field in the second quarter on his first attempt at punt coverage in the NFL. He was obliterated.

"I was up there watching the game with the fans—the 49ers had blocked me that well," Mike says. "They had knocked me out of bounds as far they could."

Things didn't go any better at linebacker, where Mike played extensively in the second half. The 49ers were in their prime, having won the Super Bowl in two of the past three seasons. With so many rookies playing for the Raiders, there were frequent mix-ups in defensive calls. On one such occasion, Mike hurriedly got into his stance only to find himself sitting in front of an offensive guard. This was no place to be for a 220-pound outside linebacker.

"They run a lead play, and that guard took me for a ride for about 10 yards," Mike recalls. "Then he pancaked me. (*Translation:* Mike was knocked off his feet.) I'm thinking, 'Man, this is going to look terrible on film.' "

The Raiders played Miami in their second preseason game. Mike got a sack, forced a fumble, and had several other tackles. "I could feel myself getting better," Mike now says.

His teammates noticed the same improvements. After the sack and forced fumble, Mike headed for the sidelines in a state of great excitement. The first person to greet him on the sidelines was safety Ronnie Lott, in the final stages of his Hall of Fame career.

"He gives me a high five. He gives me a hug," Mike recalls.

And words of encouragement: *"Great play. Keep on playing."*

"After that, I started getting confidence," Mike says.

Some nerve-wracking days lay ahead for Mike as the final roster cuts loomed. The Raiders closed the preseason with a Friday night game at San Diego. As visiting team, the Raiders were reduced to using the baseball locker room. Perhaps about 40 players were squeezed inside. About two dozen others, mainly rookies and scrubs (including Mike), dressed in a back room.

"We're all dressing back there, and one of the guys says, 'Man, everybody back here is going to get cut,' " Mike recalls. Everyone in the room flinched at the mere thought of impending unemployment.

Mike didn't play against the Chargers until the fourth quarter—typically not a good sign—but he did recover a fumble. Then it was back to L.A. to wait out the final cuts. Mike heard nothing on Saturday. Or Sunday. On Monday, he returned to the Raiders' complex for a team meeting.

"I'm sitting in the meeting, and every time the door opens I turn around to see if somebody's coming to get me," Mike says. "I'm thinking, *Worst-case scenario, they're going to come and get me at the last minute.*"

Welcome to the NFL

The Raiders had until 4 P.M. to make their final cuts. Mike sweated out the hours, the minutes, the seconds that day. It seemed like 4 P.M. would never arrive.

At 2 P.M., the Raiders gathered on the field for a light workout. Star running back Marcus Allen walked by Mike and said: *"Congratulations on making the team."*

Mike: "I ain't made the team yet."

Allen: "You don't think you can still get cut, do you?"

Mike: "I thought that cut was at 4 o'clock."

Allen: "That's 4 o'clock Eastern *time, Mike."*

Since it was after 2 o'clock in L.A., it was a little after 5 P.M. Eastern time. Mike Jones had made his first NFL roster.

As a linebacker.

6

Wearing the Silver and Black

When Mike left Columbia for his first Raiders training camp in July 1991, he left without Misty. "We separated after I left Mizzou," Mike says. "I went to California, and she went back to Kansas City."

Mike speaks about this part of his life with difficulty. In a life full of achievement and success, this is a rare case of something that didn't go right. Mike and Misty married young and experienced their share of pressures and hardships bringing two children into the world during Mike's days at Mizzou.

"It was just a situation where we went our separate ways," Mike says. "I think that's the best way to put it. I tell everybody that it was my fault, and I leave it at that. It was nothing Misty did. It was nothing I did. It was just a situation where it didn't work out. And I take full responsibility for it.

"She's a great mother, and she's doing

great now. She's remarried, and her husband's a great guy. He takes care of Taelor and Moriah really well. So she's got somebody that she deserves."

Despite the current positives, that first year or two in Los Angeles with the Raiders had to include some lonely times for Mike. No doubt he missed his daughters, and perhaps he wondered what had gone wrong with his marriage. In addition, there were family concerns in Kansas City. Mike's mother, Mary Jo, suffered a brain aneurysm in 1991 (and another in 1993). So Mike found himself relying heavily on his faith and trust in God during those early days in Los Angeles.

During all this personal turmoil, Mike also had to worry about keeping his job. Unlike other professional sports, there are very few guaranteed contracts in the National Football League. The only guaranteed money usually comes in the form of signing bonuses. Despite making the team, professional football players usually have to "sing for their supper." If they don't perform, they get cut. And if they get cut, they lose most of the money in their contracts. Obviously, it helped that Mike had Raiders owner Al Davis in his corner. But as a converted running back trying to make it as a linebacker, Mike could take nothing for granted at the start of his career.

Passion and Intensity

Even as Mike was taking his first awkward steps as an NFL linebacker, those around him noticed something special about his attitude and approach. "I think the best thing about him was his intensity," Al Davis says. "His intensity was excellent."

"I don't know that I can ever remember a guy who was that committed and had that kind of fresh, unselfish attitude toward professional football," Mike White says. A Raiders assistant at the time Mike was starting out, White was head coach during Mike's last two seasons with the Silver & Black.

"He really wanted to be a good football player, and he would do whatever it took to become a good football player," says Ronnie Lott, Mike's teammate during the 1991 and 1992 seasons. "That's why he was able to hang around. He was really passionate about succeeding and being good. Just like any rookie, he had his tough times, but he didn't get discouraged by that."

The "tough times" for Mike began with the opening kickoff of the 1991 regular season—his first in the NFL. The Raiders opened with the Houston Oilers (who later moved to Nashville and became the Tennessee Titans). All during meetings that week, the veterans cautioned the rookies about the speed of the game.

"I'm thinking, *It can't be much faster than that first preseason game,*" Mike recalls. It was another lesson Mike would learn the hard way. Playing on the kickoff return team, Mike proved to be little more than a speed bump for the determined Oilers.

"I don't think I blocked a guy the whole day," Mike says. "I was horrible." So were the rest of the Raiders as Houston romped to a 47–17 victory. The following Monday, Steve Ortmayer, who doubled as special teams coach, lectured Mike about the need to play better.

There were occasional setbacks, but Mike took Ortmayer's advice to heart. He improved week by week, both on special teams and at linebacker. In fact, this first season was basically Mike's apprenticeship at linebacker. For example, during training camp, Mike was regularly assigned to cover premier running backs Marcus Allen and Roger Craig. The theory was that if Mike could cover Allen and Craig out of the backfield, he could cover anyone.

And Allen and Craig weren't the only stars on this Raiders team, which was just one season removed from participating in the AFC championship game. The roster also included Ronnie Lott and Howie Long, among others. Almost to a man, they made Mike feel at home. More important, they made him feel like his contributions were important to the team, even though he wasn't a frontline player. In addition, linebackers Jerry Robinson and Winston Moss helped tutor Mike on the finer points of the position.

"In some places the veterans turn their backs on you," Mike says. "That didn't happen there."

Early in the season, the Raiders slotted Mike as a coverage linebacker for use in passing situations. About midway through the season, Mike began seeing duty in "nickel" and "dime" packages (personnel groupings designed to stop the pass). In addition to his playing time at linebacker and on return coverage, Mike received plenty of work at strong safety, normally the domain of smaller, faster players. Again, this sharpened his coverage skills. Even in conditioning drills, Mike always ran with wide receivers Willie Gault and Sam Graddy, both former Olympic sprinters.

As the end of the season neared, the Raiders found themselves in contention for a playoff spot. Veteran Jerry Robinson was moved into Mike's linebacker role in the nickel and dime defenses. Mike's playing time was limited to special teams once again.

Around the World (League)

After a 9–7 regular season, capped by a

wild-card playoff loss to Kansas City, Al Davis decided to accelerate Mike's learning process. In spring 1992, Davis assigned Mike to play for the Sacramento Surge of the World League, a developmental league for younger players.

"At first, he wasn't sure if he wanted to do it," Davis recalls. "And then I was sure he didn't want to do it when I said, 'We're going to play you at middle linebacker.' "

Mike was undersized even for an outside linebacker, which was his NFL position. Why move him inside to middle linebacker where size and strength were even more desirable? "What I wanted him to do was develop the toughness on the inside," Davis explains. In addition, even when Mike was playing in obvious passing situations for the Raiders, he frequently would have to patrol the middle. Davis wanted to acclimate him to playing on that part of the field.

"I flew up to Sacramento about three times to watch him play," Davis remembers. "And I started to get excited about him because I could see that he was a leader on the field, and he could run."

Davis may have been excited, but Sacramento defensive coordinator Jim Haslett wasn't exactly doing cartwheels when the Raiders sent Mike his way. "Al had given us a bunch of guys the year before, and none of them really panned out," Haslett recalls. "In Mike's first year with the Raiders, he wasn't really doing anything. He was just kind of running around on special teams. And then Al Davis called and said, 'I'm going to send you a guy. He's a fullback. I'm trying to make him a linebacker. He's not real big. He's not real tall. He's fast, but he doesn't weigh a lot.' And I'm thinking, *'Oh great, another one of those guys.'* "

Truth be told, Mike wasn't exactly doing cartwheels when he learned of his World League assignment. "I didn't want to do it at first because I'd just played my rookie NFL season, and I wanted to get a little down time," Mike says. "Then I thought, *'It'll give me some playing experience. Besides, the Raiders stuck out their necks for me to learn how to play the position.'* "

So Mike's "off-season" ended in February when he reported to the Surge. The team's two-week training camp took place in San Marcos, Texas. Accommodations were several steps short of luxurious. "The hotel we stayed in was a dump," Mike says bluntly. "A Motel 6 was a five-star hotel compared to it."

One word best described the training table food in San Marcos: predictable. "Every day we would have turkey," Mike remembers. "It would be turkey and some kind of potato. Turkey and a baked potato. Turkey and mashed potatoes. One day, they said they were going to switch up and have Salisbury steak. They covered up the steak with a whole bunch of mashed potatoes and gravy."

After a couple of bites, Mike thought the meat tasted funny and decided to investigate. He scraped off the potatoes and gravy and held the meat up for inspection. "It was turkey," Mike says with a laugh. "I still haven't figured that one out."

And to top it off the conditions in Sacramento were spartan. All 37 members of the Surge lived in the same apartment building. All of them made the same base salary—$25,000—or less than half the NFL minimum wage at that time. This was good for team morale, but it was no way to get rich.

At least the Surge didn't turn out to be a bunch of turkeys. With a roster that included the now-famous "pro" wrestler Goldberg, who played defensive tackle, Sacramento finished 8–2 in the regular season. They went on to defeat Barcelona and Orlando in the playoffs to claim the league championship. Mike missed three games with a knee injury, but otherwise the season was a huge success.

"Mike wasn't hard to teach," Haslett recalls. "He just has football instincts. That was the big thing you saw in him. Obviously, he could run and he could cover. And the other thing that was impressive, he was very intelligent. So it wasn't hard for him to pick it up. He was kind of the leader of the defense. He just took over as an inside linebacker.

"The only thing I wondered about back then was how far he could go because he's not the biggest guy in the world. But he overcame whatever limitations he had with smarts and speed."

Even the knee injury proved to be a blessing in disguise. After he returned to the lineup, Mike twinged the knee against the Ohio Glory. With the Surge comfortably ahead on the scoreboard, Mike looked to the sidelines, trying to get Haslett's attention so a replacement could be sent into the game. Haslett ignored Mike.

When the defensive series was over, Mike approached Haslett on the sidelines. "I know you're mad at me," Haslett remembers telling Mike. "I know your knee is hurting, but we had to leave you in there because if you want to come out every time you've got a little nick, you're not going to get over that injury."

Mike played the rest of the game and learned a lesson about playing with pain and discomfort. It's a fact of life in the NFL, which illustrates the gladiator aspect of the sport. As Dick Vermeil used to say as coach of the St. Louis Rams, the last day a football player felt 100 percent healthy was the first day of training camp.

"It did help me," Mike now says, referring to Haslett's decision in the Sacramento-Ohio game. "After I had that little nick, whenever I'd get nicked up, I was able to play through it. I wouldn't think about just running off the field and getting somebody to step in for me."

The World League championship game, known as the World Bowl, proved to be a good dress rehearsal for Super Bowl XXXIV. Before 44,000 fans at Montreal's Olympic Stadium, Sacramento defeated Orlando 21–17. Proving he is no stranger to big plays in big games, Mike set up the winning touchdown by intercepting a Scott Mitchell pass midway through the fourth quarter. Following the game, Surge players, coaches, and officials were guests of honor at a parade in Sacramento. As co-captain of the team, along with quarterback David Archer, Mike addressed the crowd. Later, the players received World League championship rings.

"The World League was a great experience," Mike says. "It taught me how to read offensive linemen a whole lot better because I had to do it as a middle linebacker." Mike improved his run defense immeasurably, and his general confidence level in playing the linebacker position increased as well.

A Step Backward

For NFL players, one of the biggest down-sides to a World League stint is the lack of an off-season. Following the World Bowl triumph and the victory parade in Sacramento, Mike returned home to Missouri in mid-June. One month later, he was back in training camp with the Raiders on the West Coast.

As is frequently the case for World League veterans, Mike started fast in his return to the NFL, but he gradually wore down over the course of the season. "When I got to training camp with the Raiders, I was already in football shape. I was already used to banging," Mike says. "I had very little soreness. The first pre-season game against the 49ers, I played like a quarter and a half, and I had something like 11 tackles."

Mike continued to improve his play early in the 1992 regular season. "But I hit a wall about week number 6," Mike remembers. "No matter what I did, I was just totally tired. Instead of getting better, I was just trying to get through the season."

Mike began that 1992 season with the Raiders playing some goal-line and third-down defense at linebacker. But as his stamina deteriorated, so did his playing time. By the end of the season, Mike was reduced to playing only special teams. "My second season wasn't good at all," Mike says. "I was just fortunate I didn't get injured."

So in the short run, the World League experience hindered Mike's NFL career. But in the long run, it paid huge dividends. "You could see the difference in me being a linebacker from the time I started with the Raiders to playing in the World League," Mike says. "That was only a year, but it was night and day compared to where I started."

More improvement was necessary, but Mike had made dramatic strides.

Help from the Top

During Mike's struggles in 1992, Al Davis was never far away. In fact, Davis may have been too close to suit some of the Raiders' defensive coaches. On more than one occasion at practice, Mike would trot out to join the first-team defense at linebacker. Defensive coordinator Gunther Cunningham would bark out, *"What are you doing out here? We didn't call the second-team defense."*

Mike would point to the sidelines where Davis, the Raiders' owner, was standing. *"Oh, okay,"* Cunningham would say, and Mike would stay on the field.

Davis had instructed Mike to get out there

with the starters. "They call that *meddling,*" Davis says, poking fun at himself. "I stopped doing that. We used to do it with several people. It's very difficult [dealing] with coaches. Besides a coach, they want to be a general manager. My whole approach was: 'You coach 'em. Let me worry about their growth.'

"You always hear coaches tell players: 'You're making a mistake. Don't make mistakes.' My approach is: 'Just win. Let your talents win. Don't worry about making mistakes. You're going to make mistakes. Mistakes are normal. You can't dwell on it. You've got to go on.' "

A Breakthrough Year

Mike listened to his mentor and played through his mistakes. After spending the entire off-season resting and training, Mike was primed from the start of training camp in 1993. So were his teammates. They were determined to regain their winning ways after a disappointing 7–9 campaign in 1992.

"When we started training camp, it was an all-out war," Mike remembers. "It was very competitive the first two weeks, unlike any other time I was with the Raiders. We practiced in full pads for a like a week straight. So tempers were flying. The first day, we had fights."

Once emotions cooled, the Raiders bonded as a team. Although Mike played for several Raiders squads that were more talented, none played better as a team. And as a team, the Raiders gained a measure of success. The 1993 Raiders finished the regular-season 10–6, and for the first time since 1991, the team entered post-season play. But after defeating Denver 42–24 in a wild-card playoff game, the Raiders lost to Buffalo 29–23 in an AFC semifinal matchup.

Mike benefited from a familiar face as linebackers coach for the Raiders during the season—Jim Haslett. Mike's former defensive coordinator in the World League stayed with the Raiders for the 1994 season as well, helping Mike further polish his linebacking skills.

"Mike just kept improving," Haslett says. "Every year you saw it—he got better and better. He's the most instinctive guy that I've ever been around as a linebacker. The best thing he does is probably covering a receiver. He can go out and cover a wideout. He can cover a running back. He just has better man-to-man skills than anybody."

The 1993 season proved to be a breakthrough year for Mike Jones—it was the year he went from experiment to bona fide NFL player. He became the Raiders' official nickel linebacker, playing in obvious passing situations and on the team's goal-line defense.

Mike and Leslie

For Mike, 1993 was a breakthrough year in more ways than one. After his marriage to Misty ended in 1992, Mike needed to rebuild that portion of his life. He began to spend more and more time with Leslie, a friend he had made while attending the University of Missouri.

Leslie remembers that Mike was late for one particular date in February 1993. "I was so upset with him," she recalls. "I'd been ready for a couple of hours, and he hadn't shown up."

Near the end of dinner, Leslie discovered the reason for Mike's delay of game. He cleared his throat and pulled out an engagement ring, saying, "This is something I've been wanting to do for a long time."

Mike had been late that evening because he was out looking for just the right ring. "You know how we do it," Mike explains. "We wait till the last minute." (*We*, of course, refers to the male of the species.)

Mike and Leslie were married in St. Louis on June 12, 1993.

"Michael's a very, very, very caring person," Leslie says. "And that's what attracted me in the beginning. His heart is so big, as I've told him, to a fault. He won't turn anybody down. That's why God put us together—because Michael tells me I'm a 'meanie.' I say, 'I'm not a meanie, but you can't tell everybody yes.'

"So I think God put us together to balance each other out because Michael will give his last dime if it's helping somebody. I say, 'That would be wonderful and fine. But guess what? You have three children and a fourth on the way.' " (They have a daughter, Ashley, and are expecting another child in July 2000.)

Changes

Following that strong 1993 campaign, the Raiders were being touted as Super Bowl contenders in 1994. But the team couldn't quite recover from a 1–3 start. With a 9–6 record, the Raiders needed to beat Mike's hometown team, the Kansas City Chiefs, in the final game of the regular season to qualify for the playoffs. But as was so often the case during Mike's tenure with the Raiders, Kansas City got the best of it. The final score was 19–9.

This proved to be Art Shell's last game as Raiders head coach. He was fired after a six-year run in which he posted a respectable 56–41 record. It also proved to be the Raiders final game in Los Angeles. Just a few months after the Rams announced they were moving from

L.A. to St. Louis for the 1995 season, Davis let it be known he was returning the Raiders to their original home—Oakland.

Small-World Department: Mike was hardly a man about town, but he enjoyed living in L.A. He went to the beach, to Disneyland, to Lakers basketball games. Occasionally, he'd run into a celebrity. More often he ran into members of the Rams' organization—some of whom would become future teammates in St. Louis. He met Toby Wright, a Rams safety from 1994–98, and Roman Phifer, a Rams linebacker from 1991–98. Mike also remembers getting the best of D'Marco Farr, at the time a rookie, in a 1994 Raiders-Rams pre-season game at Anaheim Stadium. "He's playing on the punt team, and I'd get him every time," Mike recalls. "I blocked a punt on him. That's my first blocked punt."

The changes just kept coming for Mike Jones and the Raiders as they entered the 1995 season. Mike White was promoted to head coach, and free agency opened up competition in the linebacker ranks. During the off-season Mike's one-time tutor at outside linebacker, Winston Moss, signed a free-agent contract with the Seattle Seahawks. This opened the door for Mike.

The competition for Moss' job consisted of Rob Holmberg, a seventh-round draft pick in 1994 from Penn State, and rookie Mike Morton, a fourth-round draft pick from North Carolina. Mike probably won the starting job with a strong performance against the St. Louis Rams in the second preseason game of 1995. "I had a sack, about seven tackles, and like three tackles for loss," Mike remembers. Preseason game or not, it was an historic occasion. In the first Raiders game played in Oakland since 1981, the Raiders defeated the former Los Angeles Rams 27–22.

During that 1995 season, no one really told Mike he was the starter. Week after week, he kept seeing his name listed at the top of the depth chart. He just kept making the plays, doing his job, and his name kept showing up. But he also had an ally in head coach Mike White, who had been on the Raiders' staff since 1990.

"Mike and I sort of immediately hit it off because of the Missouri-Illinois rivalry," White recalls. (White had been head coach at the University of Illinois during Mike's first two seasons at Mizzou. Although the colleges never played each other in football during Mike's time in Columbia, they had—and continue to have—a spirited rivalry in basketball.)

Small-World Department: In addition to the connection created by the Missouri-Illinois rivalry, Mike White and Mike Jones also have some mutual friends—including Jimmy Collins, who had played for Coach White at Illinois before transferring to Mizzou in 1988.

"Mike and I immediately hit it off and developed a relationship," White says. "His wife, Leslie, and my wife [Marilyn] sort of pioneered getting the wives of the players and coaches together and involved. The Raiders had never, ever, done anything like that. That was never one of their approaches, as you might guess. They sort of prided themselves on being rebels and stuff."

Over their years together with the Raiders, White spent almost all of his time coaching offense, even as a head coach. But he couldn't help noticing Mike's development as a linebacker. "He wasn't a guy that knocked your eyes out initially because he was learning the business," White says. "But he was a guy that had tremendous speed and, obviously, athletic ability."

Because the franchise move was finalized so late in the summer, the Raiders basically commuted to Oakland during the 1995 season. The team practiced in Los Angeles during the week, and the players and coaches kept their homes or apartments in L.A. But the day before each "home" game, the team would fly from L.A. to Oakland and stay overnight in a hotel.

"At first it was great," Mike says. "We started off on fire. But we knew it was going to catch up with us. If you play 16 road games, it's going to catch up with you." And it did catch up with them over the second half of the season, as did injuries to quarterback Jeff Hostetler. After an 8–2 start, the Raiders collapsed down the stretch to finish 8–8.

Although Mike remained a Raider, he established a permanent residence in St. Louis in 1995 when he and Leslie bought a house in suburban University City. When the Raiders formally moved to Oakland in 1996, the Joneses rented an apartment there as well.

Early that May, Leslie remained in St. Louis, awaiting the birth of their first child. Mike planned to leave the Raiders' off-season conditioning program a day or two early to surprise his wife. Leslie ended up surprising him. Leslie went into labor early, and Mike ended up catching a red-eye flight to St. Louis. He arrived in time to witness the birth of daughter Ashley on May 2.

Ashley may have arrived early, but the

Raiders started late in 1996. After a 1–4 start, they won their next three games to even their slate at 4–4. But they lost the following week by a point to Denver, 22–21. Next came back-to-back overtime losses to Tampa Bay and Minnesota. It was an excruciating stretch in what became an excruciating season. The Raiders would finish with a 7–9 record, costing White his head-coaching job. Eight of those nine losses were by a touchdown or less.

Small-World Department: Mike White moved from his head-coaching gig with the Raiders to a position as one of Dick Vermeil's assistants with the St. Louis Rams almost immediately. White, a longtime friend of the Rams' new head coach, was instrumental in getting Vermeil to consider bringing Mike Jones to St. Louis.

Home Cooking

"The only thing good about that [1996] season was that I finally beat Kansas City again," Mike says. "I hadn't beaten Kansas City in years."

When Oakland beat the visiting Chiefs 26–7 in a Monday night game on December 9, 1996, it marked only the second victory over Kansas City in 13 tries during Mike's six-year stay with the

Raiders. Included in the setbacks was a 10–6 loss at Arrowhead Stadium in 1991, Mike's first playoff game. And there was that 19–9 loss in L.A. to close the 1994 season, which cost the Raiders a playoff berth and Art Shell his job. Mike also played his first Monday night game against the Chiefs, a 24–21 loss at Arrowhead in 1991.

"They [Kansas City] just found a way to win games against the Raiders," Mike says. "I don't know how they did it, but they always found a way to beat us."

Many of Mike's hometown friends in Kansas City delighted in pointing out the lopsided nature of this heated AFC West rivalry. "A lot of my friends were Chiefs fans, but they were also Mike Jones fans," Mike says. "If it came down to it, they were Mike Jones fans. Of course, they were going to razz me because I couldn't beat the home team."

Things weren't any easier for Mike's family. When the Raiders made their annual trip to Kansas City, the Jones family showed up at Arrowhead wearing Raiders garb. "It was tough because we would get a lot of harassment at the stadium," says Mike's brother Kevin. "I just wasn't used to being in Kansas City and having fans booing you and throwing stuff at you." In fact, Leroy Sr. sometimes would stay in the parking lot, waiting for Chiefs fans to enter the stadium first so he could avoid possible confrontations.

It was tough being a Raiders fan in a Chiefs town, but that didn't prevent the Jones family from extending their own personal brand of hospitality to the Raiders. When the Raiders came to town, Mike would bring 10 or 15 teammates home with him the night before the game for some home cooking. They'd munch on barbecue ribs, fried chicken, macaroni and cheese—among other Jones family specialities.

"We'd have everything," sister Jan remembers. "What didn't we have, that's the question."

Leroy Sr.'s beans were a particular favorite with the Raiders. Chester McGlockton, Jerry Ball, Vince Evans, Greg Biekert, James Folston, and Mike Morton were just some of the Raiders who sampled those beans from time to time.

Kansas City's trademark hospitality was otherwise absent during Raiders visits. In a 1996 visit, Arrowhead Stadium was unavailable for the Raiders' normal "walk-through" practice the day before the game. The Raiders were forced to board buses and work out at a local high school field.

After practice, Mike remembers sitting on the last bus, waiting to head back to the team hotel. And waiting. And waiting. "As a joke, someone paid the bus driver to leave," Mike recalls. "We're sitting there for like 30 minutes; the bus driver doesn't show up. So we walk around, trying to find out where he is."

The keys were in the ignition, but the driver couldn't be found. Finally, place-kicker Cole Ford got behind the wheel and commandeered the bus. As Mike remembers it, the world should be thankful that Ford had a more suitable vocation.

"If you've ever driven a bus, you know you can accidentally sideswipe a stop sign," Mike says. "Cole didn't sideswipe one; he took it out of the ground. He didn't judge it right. I told him, 'Whatever you do, just get us back to the hotel in one piece.'"

Farewell Raiders

Mike didn't make it through the 1996 season in one piece. He suffered a hip pointer, or bruised hip, against Denver in the second-to-last game of the season. The injury forced him to sit out the season finale against Seattle. That marked the first, and only, game Mike has missed in his nine-year NFL career.

Despite missing that last game, no one could deny that Mike Jones had become a solid NFL starter. He led the Raiders in tackles in 1995 and shared the team lead with Greg Biekert in

1996, even though he missed that Seattle game. But Mike's contract was up following the '96 season, and the Raiders had made no move to re-sign him.

"When the season ended, I was joking with Chester and Tim Brown and the guys: 'It's been real nice playing with you guys,' " Mike recalls.

A lot of Mike's relatives came out to Oakland for Christmas in 1996. Not knowing for sure if he'd be back with the Raiders, Mike did some sightseeing in the Bay Area in early January—Alcatraz, Fisherman's Wharf.

It proved to be time well spent.

Mike during his grade-school days at St. Augustine's.

Mike's eighth-grade graduation photo.

The Jones family affectionately call Kim, Monica (back, from left), Maria, Mark, and Mike (front, from left) "Roots II" because the older four Jones children were already teenagers when these five family members were born.

Photos courtesy of the Jones family.

Mike's Little League team. He's the fifth player from the left in the back row. Mike's best friend, Kenny White, is below him in the middle row.

Mike as a member of the St. Augustine's baseball team. He was 7 years old.

Mike and James Garrett ready to attend a homecoming dance.

Mike (back row, far left) with one of the teams he helped coach. Kenny White is standing at the far right in the back row.

Photos courtesy of the Jones family.

*Mike in his days as a running back with
the University of Missouri Tigers.*

Photo courtesy of University of Missouri—Columbia, Athletic Department.

Mike and daughter Taelor. She was a regular member of the Breakfast Crew during Mike's days at Mizzou.

Photo courtesy of the Jones family.

*Mike and family members
celebrate the baptism
of Taelor and Moriah.
Mike chose friend Darren
Fulcher (front row, left) to
be godfather for both girls.*
Photos courtesy of the Jones family.

Above: The Jones family—(back row) Kevin, Kim, Maria, Jan, Mark, Monica, and Mike; (front row) Patti, Leroy Sr., Mary Jo, and Leroy Jr. Below: Mike and his brothers with Leroy Sr. Both of these pictures were taken at Mary Jo's retirement party.

*Mike Jones working with attendees at
one of his free football camps.*
Photo courtesy of St. Louis Rams.

Photo courtesy of Bill Stover, photographer, St. Louis.

Mike with students at Our Lady of Angels in suburban St. Louis.

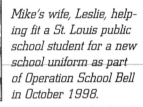

Mike's wife, Leslie, helping fit a St. Louis public school student for a new school uniform as part of Operation School Bell in October 1998.

Mike and Leslie standing with gifts received during the Angel Tree campaign in 1999. These gifts answered "wish lists" from needy families.

Photos courtesy of St. Louis Rams.

Mike posing with children attending a 1999 holiday party at Rams Park for children in foster care.

Rams defensive end Kevin Carter and Mike before the start of a charity softball game in 1999.

Photos courtesy of St. Louis Rams.

Photo courtesy of Bill Stover, photographer, St. Louis.

Speaking to a student assembly in 1998 at Mann Elementary School in St. Louis.

Photo courtesy of St. Louis Rams.

Heading to Atlanta, Mike caught up on the coverage of the NFC championship game with Tampa Bay.

Returning to his room after the Super Bowl, Mike enjoyed watching a replay of The Tackle.

Mike flashes a number 1 in celebration of the Rams' victory.

Rams owner Georgia Frontiere presents Mike with his Super Bowl ring at a ceremony in June 2000.

Photos courtesy of Bill Stover, photographer, St. Louis.

7

A Lifestyle of Giving
Begins at Home

Let's take a timeout in our review of Mike Jones' football career and step back in time to early February 1993. Mike had just completed his second season with the Raiders. He and his then-girlfriend, Leslie, were in Kansas City, visiting friends at the home of Marvin Fight, one of Mike's teammates from his days at Southwest High. They played cards and dominoes, talked over old times, and caught up on new developments. Several members of the old group were around, including Kenny White, Mike's "first best friend."

Mike and Leslie headed back to St. Louis the next day. But roughly 36 hours after that get-together at Marvin Fight's, Mike was jolted by a phone call from Kansas City.

"Once he got the phone call, he just held the phone," Leslie recalls. "I was like: 'What? What?' "

Kenny White had been shot and killed the night before.

"Kenny was a very good kid," recalls Mike's mother, Mary Jo. "Very nice, well-mannered. Respectful. He'd come over, and they'd play every day, he and Mike. If they weren't playing baseball or football out on the front yard, they were playing 'army' or something."

But by the time Mike was finishing high school, Kenny had begun to hang out with the wrong crowd. "He had a cousin that was making bad choices, and Kenny was right there with him," Mary Jo says. "Kenny wasn't going to college or anything, so their choices were traveling and doing the wrong things."

Kenny got in some trouble in Atlanta. The Jones family thinks it was drug-related. He ended up doing jail time in Georgia.

"Some of my friends were going the wrong way, and they were going the wrong way fast," Mike recalls. "And some guys were going the wrong way, but they were able to turn it around. It's kind of strange."

Among a group of 10 close friends, Mike included, five graduated from high school and went on to lead productive lives. But the other five didn't graduate from high school. This group included Kenny White. And this group often found trouble. "It was like two extremes,"

Mike says.

In Kenny's case, he got out of jail around the time Mike completed his first season with the Raiders. "I think jail really scared him," Mary Jo says, "because he went out and got a good job."

About a year later, Kenny showed up at a neighborhood party on February 13, 1993, and bumped into an old nemesis. "Kenny and the guy had been feuding before," Mike says. "Somehow, someway, both of them ended up at the same party. They got into a little argument and were separated. They got into another argument and were separated."

Somehow, the antagonists ended up outside. "They got into another argument," Mike says. "One of them pulled a gun on the other, and they started shooting."

Kenny was shot once and ran off into the night. The next day, he was found lying dead by a fence in Mrs. Hart's yard—the same yard where Mike, Kenny, and the other neighborhood kids had spent countless carefree hours playing basketball. Authorities think Kenny started losing blood, got winded, and got caught up on the fence. He passed out and died in the cold February darkness.

After Mike got the phone call from Kansas City, Leslie says, "He was just kind of in a daze the rest of the day. That was his best friend. We had just been with him." And now Kenny was gone.

After the funeral, Mike and several of his old neighborhood friends gathered at the home of Mike's brother Kevin. They cooked and played cards and reminisced about Kenny. "Later on that evening, they were all standing out in the yard. They were talking about Kenny, and they all broke down crying," Kevin says. "Just all of them cried like a baby right there in my front yard."

Remembering Kenny

Basically, it was then and there that the Michael Jones Foundation came into existence. "Michael had always said that he wanted to give something back," Leslie says. "It was just a matter of doing it. When we were coming back to St. Louis [from Kenny's funeral], he said, 'I need to go ahead and do something now. Maybe I can stop some of these other kids from going down the wrong path. I've put it off long enough.'

"His friend had died a senseless death, just from what I call stupidity and people not being able to handle their temper. It was kind of like his jump start, his motivator, to do something."

There was organizational work to do. First, nonprofit status was achieved for the foundation. Then, the first of Mike's free football camps and fund-raising events took place in the spring and summer of 1994.

A Family Affair

From the start, the Michael Jones Foundation wasn't a matter of Mike making a cameo appearance, writing a check, then going on about his business. And his activities have only increased since his move to the St. Louis Rams. "A lot of players are involved in the community, but no one is as hands-on involved as Mike," says Marci Moran, who runs the Rams' community relations department. "A lot of guys who have foundations hire people to run it for them. Usually the guy shows up, takes all the glory, and then they disappear."

Not so with Mike. At his most recent charity auction, he was seen setting up auction items and lugging in soft drinks before the event. During the foundation's annual Christmas toy drive, Mike not only picks up the toys, he personally hands them out to the kids. When it's time for one of his charity football camps, he loads the equipment—footballs, tackling dummies, blocking pads, and cones—into the back of his pickup and off he goes.

But it's not a solo act.

"It really is a family affair," Moran says. "Leslie's there. His parents are there. His in-laws are there. His siblings are there. Leslie's siblings are around. They're really supportive. With a lot of players, when they start a foundation, they use it to pay their family members' salaries, which can be written off. But Michael's deal is they're all volunteers."

Nobody gets a dime. So why do they do it? "Because he's my baby brother," sister Jan says, laughing.

But there's more to it than that. "A lot of it comes from our parents," Jan says. "They've always been involved in everything. Our schools. Church. They've kind of pushed their skills off on us."

Jan and another sister, Patti, run the Kansas City camp. Leslie runs the St. Louis camp. Brother Kevin helps line up coaches and helps Mike with transportation of equipment and setup. Mary Jo and Leroy attend as many camps as possible, handing out T-shirts and sport drinks to the participants.

In the past, Mike has expressed a desire to enter coaching when his playing days are over. He looks the part at his camps. "He's really intense," Patti says. "His love for football really comes through. And he's really, really good with the kids."

It's not as if Mike hasn't done this before. As a high schooler in Kansas City he helped his mentor, Clarence Stephenson, coach the younger kids in the area youth sports program. "So he's kind of used to giving that training and has that authoritative manner," Patti says. "But he still has a lot of fun with it."

There's usually much more to a Mike Jones camp than just football. The typical camp in Kansas City starts on Wednesday with a special needs camp for the physically or mentally challenged, which was the idea of Keith Hannaman, Mike's football coach at Southwest High. The regular camp is Thursday, Friday, and Saturday. Children ages 5 and up are welcome. Speakers come in regularly to talk to the campers about aiming high, staying in school, the dangers of gang violence, and saying no to drugs. Sometimes the speakers are Mike's teammates or other NFL players. Sometimes they're local doctors, lawyers, or judges. The Saturday session is Family Day, and parents are invited. Mike tells the parents what the kids have learned during the camp. T-shirts and bags are handed out. Hot dogs, soda, chips, and cookies are served. And Jan and Leroy Sr. usually do the cooking.

Branching Out

Near the end of the 1997 Rams' season, David Johnson was sitting in his office at a youth center in Columbia, Missouri. As executive director of the new Columbia Boys and Girls Club, he was trying to get some things organized.

"Next thing you know, one of my staff partners said, 'There's a person that wants to talk to you,' " Johnson recalls. "So I go through my door, and I see this big fellow. Solid muscle, 240 pounds.

"I'm thinking, 'Okay, what parent did I upset? What kid did I suspend from the club.' I'm thinking hard, when this fellow says, 'Hi, my name is Mike Jones. I play with the St. Louis Rams. I'd like to come in and run a football clinic for your kids.' "

Johnson couldn't believe his ears. "I'm like, 'Okay, no problem. Come in and have a seat in my office. Can I get you anything to drink?' "

In Johnson's line of work, it's usually not that easy. But from that very first conversation, Johnson recalls, "You could tell this was a very sincere person who really cared about kids and wanted to really give back. Ever since, it's really been a great relationship."

Mike has had football camps in Columbia since 1997. Since 1999, he also has hosted a charity basketball game to raise funds for the boys and girls club. He usually brings some special guests along, such as Rams defensive end Kevin Carter, tight end Roland Williams, and wide receiver Torry Holt. And they do more than just show up and smile.

Recalling the most recent special needs camp, Johnson says, "You should have seen the look on those kids' faces when those guys were working with them. The players were allowing them to tackle them and were falling down on the floor.

"Mike was sensational. He's out there playing with them, showing them how to tackle, how to kick the ball, holding the ball for field goals. It was just great to see. And the parents—I think they had bigger smiles than the kids."

And, as usual, Mike did his own heavy lifting, or at least tried to. "Mike pulls up, and he's getting the equipment off the truck for the football camp," Johnson recalls. "I'm like, 'Mike, we've got 60 volunteers out here. All you've got to do is let them know what they need to do, and they'll be happy to do it.' "

After the most recent charity basketball game, Johnson sat down with Mike and thanked him for his efforts:

Johnson: "You helped our organization make over $11,000."

Mike: "Great. I'm happy to hear that. We want to do better next year."

"I've dealt with some athletes, who in a situation like that might say, 'Okay, how much do I get, and when do I get it?' " Johnson says. In other words, they want a piece of the pie. Not Mike.

"That's just how he's always been," Johnson says. "There's never been any hidden agendas."

Continuing to Grow

Mike's work in Columbia has typified the growth of the Michael Jones Foundation in recent years. The first football camps took place in 1994 in Kansas City and St. Louis. By the spring and summer of 2000, Mike was holding camps in St. Louis, Kansas City, Columbia, and Springfield in Missouri; and in East St. Louis and Scott Air Force Base in Illinois. And keep in mind, these camps are all free of charge.

"There's a lot of players that do football camps," Moran points out. "But very few of them are free like Mike's."

And Mike even found time to add another stop on his foundation itinerary following the Super Bowl triumph: a charity basketball event in Rolla, Missouri. "If he could, he'd do a camp anywhere anybody asked him," Leslie says. "I have to tell him, 'You can't be everywhere at one time. You just can't.' Michael's spirit, Michael's heart, is so big. He hates to say no."

Attendance always has been good at the camps, but it has improved steadily year by year.

The hardest part was attracting sponsors in the early years, which meant Mike had to cover many expenses out of his pocket. The initial fund-raising efforts centered around charity basketball games in Kansas City and St. Louis. But those games didn't generate much revenue in 1994 and 1995, so in 1997, Mike went in another direction and started an annual charity golf tournament in St. Louis. An auction was added in 1998. In 1999, Mike hooked up with teammate Kevin Carter to "co-host" a charity softball game, featuring several Rams players.

Put all these events together and you have the Michael Jones Foundation Celebrity Weekend. The lineup for the 2000 event, held the first weekend in May, was as follows:

- A dinner auction on Thursday at the Rams Park indoor practice facility.
- A football camp in East St. Louis on Friday and Saturday.
- A charity softball game on Sunday against a group of media "all-stars" in St. Louis County.
- A charity golf tournament and dinner on Monday in St. Louis County.

Stressing Education and Community Involvement

In addition to the free football camps, the foundation has been awarding college scholarships to St. Louis and Kansas City area youth for the last four years. And as the foundation has grown, so has the scholarship program. Four one-year scholarships worth $1,000 apiece were awarded in years one and two of the program. In year three, eight one-year scholarships worth $1,000 apiece were awarded. The program was expanded greatly in 2000, offering 10 four-year scholarships that are worth $2,000 per year.

In addition to Leslie's work with the football camps, she also coordinates an "adopt a family" program around the Christmas holidays that invites Rams employees to provide Christmas gifts for the needy. There's also a Michael Jones Foundation toy drive.

Not directly related to the foundation is Mike's work as a spokesperson for the Family Court of St. Louis County Mentor Program. The program links delinquent youth, ages 11–16, with adult volunteers. The idea is to expose the youth to positive role models.

Mike also is considering a couple new programs, both in their creative stages. One would be an after-school program at local youth clubs that would help educate kids about politics, current events, and the importance of voting. "Then based on attendance, participation, and an essay, several kids would earn a trip to Washington, D.C.," Moran says. The other program would provide down payments on home purchases for low-income families. Mike is talking with teammate D'Marco Farr about the possibility of joining forces on such a project.

Setting the Standard

Mike is starting to gain some notoriety for his community and charitable efforts. In August 1999, he was named one of "99 Good Guys" in pro sports by *The Sporting News.* Two months after the Rams' Super Bowl victory, he received the Progressive Youth Center's World of Children Award. And he was a 1999 nominee for the prestigious NFL Man of the Year award, which recognizes off-the-field contributions by NFL players.

"Mike's a great football player, but a lot of times I think of Mike more for what he does off the football field and the things he does in the community," Rams quarterback Kurt Warner says. "He's always willing to help out in any given situation; he's going to give back to somebody in some way. I think he's just a good example for all of us."

Although very community conscious and

charity minded in his own right, Warner is still relatively new to the NFL and the forum that his sudden celebrity status can provide. He has learned from watching Mike. Warner has been particularly impressed with the variety of Mike's community and charitable efforts. "From the football camps, to the golf tournament, the softball game—it seems like any time there's a charity event with the Rams involved, that Mike's usually involved in some way, shape, or form," Warner says. "I've been very conscious of that because I would like to get to that level throughout my career."

Even with his hectic off-season in the wake of earning Super Bowl MVP and regular-season MVP honors, Warner always finds time for Mike. He made an appearance at the Michael Jones Foundation dinner auction at Rams Park and played in Mike's charity golf tournament and softball game.

"A lot of the guys recognize what Mike does and the big impact that he has," Warner says. "If we take out an hour or two hours of our day, that's nothing compared to what Mike's taking out of his time to give back to these different organizations or these kids. I think the guys realize that. That's why I'm happy to help out in any way I can." Even if it means jumping into a baby pool, which is what Warner did at the charity softball game to raise an extra $500.

The spirit of volunteerism seems to be infectious for Mike's friends, whether they've known him for five years or 15. David Johnson of the Columbia Boys and Girls Club found the time to help Mike at his 2000 football camp in East St. Louis and also attended the foundation's golf tournament and dinner. Former high school and college teammate Curtis Roberts came in from Philadelphia to help with Mike's 2000 football camp in Columbia. Another former teammate, Jimmy Collins, is "host" for Mike's St. Louis football camp at Normandy High School, where Collins is assistant football coach, as well as a counselor in the school district. Collins helps out at all of Mike's football camps. And at the Springfield camp, Mike runs into former Mizzou backfield teammate Sean Moore.

All of which adds to the enjoyment value for Mike while he's working a camp. Not that he wouldn't be there anyway. It's a lot more fun than just writing a check. "I like doing football camps," Mike says. "You can't put a price on spending time with people."

8

Hello, St. Louis

Full-fledged free agency didn't come to the NFL until 1993. It arrived only after a lengthy court battle between players and owners. It quickly became obvious that the system could be a bonanza or a boondoggle for players on the market.

The annual free-agency period starts in mid-February and always begins with a wild spending spree during the first couple of weeks. But the dollars usually dry up quickly as teams approach their league-mandated salary cap. Timing is everything. Players who wait for a better offer run the risk of being left empty-handed.

Mike felt like a frustrated fisherman in the first month of free agency during spring 1997. He had many nibbles but no bites. Cincinnati showed some interest, as did Kansas City, but nothing materialized in either city. In the early going, Miami appeared to be the most interested. On several occasions Mike was on the verge of making a free-agent visit to the Dolphins, only to have things fall through. Miami never seemed serious about making a contract offer.

"Unless they were actually going to try and sign me, there was no use going down there," Mike says. "We didn't want to be traveling all over the country to these different teams if they weren't even going to offer a serious contract."

Small-World Department: The newly transplanted *Tennessee* Oilers (gone from Houston but still two seasons away from being renamed the *Titans*) ran hot and cold on Mike—at the same time. "You talked to three different guys in their organization, they'd tell you three different things," Mike remembers. "One guy said they really liked me. One guy said they didn't like me. (I know one of their scouts didn't really care too much for me.) And one guy was lukewarm." Too bad for Tennessee that Mike signed with St. Louis. With Mike playing for the Titans in Super Bowl XXXIV, maybe the Titans would have gone home with the Lombardi Trophy instead.

And what about the Raiders? "Oakland didn't say a word," Mike says. "It was very quiet out there."

Which was puzzling. The Raiders had invested all that time and energy developing Mike as an NFL linebacker. Now, just as he was entering his prime, they appeared disinterested in re-signing him.

Mike knew the St. Louis Rams were shopping for help at linebacker, but he didn't give them much thought. "St. Louis didn't look like a good fit," Mike recalls. "They were looking for a guy to play over the tight end." Which wasn't Mike's thing. He played off the ball, in space, and excelled at coverage. In football jargon, Mike played weakside linebacker, a position manned ably in St. Louis by Roman Phifer. Although Mike had bulked up to 230 pounds, that was still on the small side for a strongside linebacker who would be expected to take on 260-pound tight ends.

As mid-March rolled around, Mike was a tad panicky. Would the free-agent parade pass him by?

Ground Zero

Dick Vermeil didn't accept the head-coaching job in St. Louis until the third week in January—the Monday of Super Bowl week, to be precise. Pete Carroll, Bobby Ross, Kevin Gilbride, and George Seifert had all said no to Rams president John Shaw before Vermeil said yes.

It was a startling choice. Vermeil had been out of coaching since 1982 when he left the Philadelphia Eagles because of burnout. The long hours, and the pressures of the game, had consumed him. Now, after 14 years in the broadcast booth as an analyst, Vermeil decided to give coaching another try by taking over the NFL's losingest team in the 1990s. The move had the potential to be sensational or disastrous.

Vermeil hit the ground running, scrambling to put together a staff after most of the top assistants in the league already had been snapped up by other clubs. He barely completed his staff in time for the start of the free-agency period. Vermeil wasn't a big fan of free agency, but he viewed it as a necessary evil, given the number of holes on the team he had inherited. Vermeil knew he had to pull some weeds on a roster that had finished 6–10 in 1996 under former head coach Rich Brooks.

"They'd been losing," Vermeil says. "And the coaches weren't the only ones that had been responsible for losing. Everyone had been losing. The personnel department, the marketing department."

And the players.

Vermeil's staff quickly came to the conclusion that they needed an upgrade at the strongside linebacker position manned by Carlos Jenkins in

1995 and 1996. Free-agent linebackers Wayne Simmons (from Green Bay) and Lewis Bush (from San Diego) were the first to visit St. Louis and meet with the Rams. Mike wasn't even on the Rams' radar screen at this point as it seemed likely that Bush would be Jenkins' replacement.

"Vermeil wanted Lew Bush," Harold Lewis, who represented Bush, recalls. "Lew had a nice meeting with them. Everything went very, very well."

But Harold Lewis knew Rams assistant head coach Mike White was trying to get Vermeil interested in Mike Jones. (White, remember, had been with the Raiders for all six of Mike's NFL seasons, so he knew Mike's strengths.) Mike Jones happened to be in St. Louis at the time of Bush's free-agent visit to Rams Park, so Harold Lewis suggested that Mike also drop by and say hello to Vermeil.

Mike didn't think that was a very good idea. He hadn't really been invited to Rams Park, and he didn't want to intrude on Bush's day with the Rams. "It just didn't seem right," Mike says.

But Harold Lewis was working all the angles. He represented both Mike Jones and Lewis Bush. One way or the other, he wanted to get one of his clients signed in St. Louis. Mike relented, stopped by Rams Park, and met with Vermeil for about five minutes.

End of story? Not even close. The next day, the Rams invited Mike to make a formal visit later in the week—the visit would include meetings, dinner, the whole works.

We Like Mike

Vermeil and several Rams assistants dined with Mike and his wife, Leslie, at a local steakhouse. The next day, Mike met with Vermeil at Rams Park. Vermeil told Mike he had polled his defensive coaches on the linebacker vacancy. Whom did they want to sign? After some film study and discussion, their answer was—Mike Jones.

Mike will never forget what happened next. "Coach Vermeil gets up and walks around his desk," Mike says. "I'm sitting in a chair. I'm wondering if he's going to escort me out of the room. So I get up, but he sticks his arms out. And I'm thinking to myself, *'I know he doesn't want to hug me.'* "

Oh, yes, he does, Mike. Oh, yes, he does.

"He gets a little teary-eyed," Mike remembers. "Then he hugs me. And he's saying, 'Yeah, you're going to be our guy.' Nothing like that had ever happened to me, not from a coach. He didn't know me. He had just met me two days ago."

But that didn't matter. Once Dick Vermeil

likes you, he *really* likes you. Make no mistake, Mike fit the Vermeil mold. But give Mike White a huge assist in getting this point across to Vermeil. "I consciously and almost dramatically told Dick: 'Here is the kind of locker room guy that we have to have to begin to be a championship team,'" White says. "'He's unselfish. He's a hard worker.'"

Vermeil was a stickler for participation in the off-season conditioning program. Because Mike's permanent home was in St. Louis, White knew he'd be around every day in the off-season, setting a good example for the younger players and the less-motivated players.

And White didn't stop his sales pitch there. He put together a highlight tape of Mike's play during the 1995 and 1996 seasons—the time period when Mike was a starter for White in Oakland. White showed it to Vermeil and the defensive coaches of the Rams. They obviously liked what they saw. "We thought Mike Jones would be a good building block, both as a player and an attitude builder," Vermeil says.

After weeks of silence, the Raiders suddenly made a late move to re-sign Mike. But it was too late. On March 18, 1997, Mike officially severed his ties with the Silver & Black and signed a four-year, $6 million contract with the Rams. The deal included a $2 million signing bonus—

money Mike received merely for signing his name on the contract. By NFL standards, it was middle-class money. But Mike clearly had come a long way from that first Raiders contract, when his signing bonus was $15,000 as an undrafted rookie.

"After I signed with the Rams, Al Davis called and left a message wishing me the best," Mike says. "He actually called my house, wishing me the best."

It was a classy gesture. Not many owners will do that after losing a player in free agency. Nonetheless, Mike can't help thinking to this day that the Raiders could have signed him back.

A part of Al Davis feels the same way. "What you look back at is *Why didn't we keep him?*" Davis says. "It's disturbing for me [because] I put in so much belief and so much hope [in Mike]."

As they had contemplated their roster for the 1997 season, the Raiders already had an established starter, Rob Frederickson, at one outside linebacker position. At the other outside linebacker spot, they had two options: re-sign Mike or go with Mike Morton.

"A decision was made to go with Morton," Davis recalls. There were cap considerations, too, because the Raiders had other free-agent priorities. But passing on Mike, Davis says, "was also a judgment, right or wrong. Obviously it wasn't right. It was a poor judgment. And I hated it."

Small-World Department: Mike Morton started 11 games for the Raiders in 1997 and 1998. Then Morton found himself a member of the St. Louis Rams in 1999—backing up Mike Jones! Following the Rams' Super Bowl triumph, Morton signed a free-agent contract with Green Bay.

A Warm Introduction

The Rams used their team auditorium to announce Mike's signing—a room traditionally used for only their bigger press conferences. Mike posed for the obligatory photos holding his new Rams jersey. Vermeil gushed about his newest roster addition.

"What we have here, and I'm not saying this just to embarrass him, we have the total package," Vermeil said at that press conference. *"He has everything that I respect, starting with talent. Number 2, he has an attitude about the game. When he makes a commitment, he makes a commitment. I will never question how hard he'll prepare to play. I will never question how hard he'll play."*

Vermeil barely knew Mike at the time. But

those words ring true today.

Vermeil then tossed a bouquet to Mike's parents by adding: *"Those qualities, his innate character traits, were ingrained in him long before he became a St. Louis Ram or an Oakland Raider."*

Clarence Stephenson, Mike's Little League coach from Kansas City, attended the press conference. He had been visiting relatives in St. Louis that weekend and decided to stay over when he learned that Mike was signing with the Rams. Asked that day what traits Mike carried over from youth to adulthood, Stephenson replied: *"Leadership. Faith in God. Ability. And everything else."*

In Oakland, the Raiders reacted graciously to the news. *"Mike is a quality person,"* team executive Bruce Allen said at the time. *"It just goes to show that if a player works hard and listens, maybe someone has a great plan for him. The truth is we also happen to be pretty deep at linebacker. Still, he made himself a real success story in this league."*

And the best was yet to come.

When Mike and Leslie headed home to University City after the press conference, their heads must have been spinning. Less than a week earlier, Mike couldn't even get a free-agent visit. Now he was a millionaire—and in his adopted hometown, no less.

"I never thought I'd end up playing here," Mike says.

Surprise, Surprise

Mike Jones' head probably was spinning again as he scanned the practice schedule the day before Rams training camp started in 1997. Mike couldn't believe his eyes. "I'm looking at it, and I'm thinking, *'Man, we're in pads a lot,'*" Mike recalls. (Full pads means more contact, which means more bumps and bruises and, potentially, more injuries.)

Then Mike looked at the part of the schedule that listed practice times—and he did a double-take. No, make that a triple-take. He remembers saying, "It looks like this says *three* hours. This has got to be a misprint. This can't be right."

It was no typo. Camp Vermeil 1997 featured 2¾-hour practices in the morning and 3-hour sessions in the afternoon. The NFL norm for a practice was about two hours, and everyone on the squad knew this.

Once camp started at Western Illinois University, Mike and his teammates quickly became aware of another problem: The Rams had more meetings than Congress. Meetings weren't ending until just minutes before the nightly 11 P.M. curfew, so Vermeil announced one day he was moving the curfew back one-half hour.

Mike and his teammates breathed a sigh of relief. At least they would have a little free time each night before turning in and doing it all over the next day. Think again. Meetings started dragging on even longer once the new curfew was instituted.

Vermeil claims there was method to his madness. "I've always felt that you had to start out tough and work harder than the players think is hard," Vermeil says. "Because you can always back off. You can always ease up."

Given the Rams losing ways, Vermeil figured the more practice time, the better. "I'm not saying the Rams were doing anything wrong before we got there," Vermeil says. "But they weren't winning, and they hadn't been winning in a long time. My first year as a head coach with the Eagles, I tried to use a very similar practice routine. The Eagles had only won four games the year before, and we didn't have a first-, second-, or third-round draft pick my first three years there. So I figured we better stay on the field. And I just kept that philosophy."

There was some grumbling about the system from the players in 1997, but they were too busy learning a new playbook—and a new coaching staff—to become overly concerned with practice schedules and meeting times.

For Mike's part, he was practically learning

a new position. Under the complex system used by Rams defensive coordinator Bud Carson, Mike was called on to do a little bit of everything—play pass defense, play run defense, rush the passer, and take on the tight end. Grappling with tight ends was grunt work, and Mike had never been asked to do it as a Raider. He always had played on the side opposite the tight end. In St. Louis, Mike was being asked to play on the tight end's side of the field as much as 60 percent of the time.

"In Oakland, Mike played off the line of scrimmage," Rams linebackers coach John Bunting explained early in the 1997 season. "He was protected by a defensive tackle, who Mike played behind probably 95 percent of the time. Mike could hide and make plays. And it was fun. Now, he's being asked to do a lot of drudgery."

And Mike was being asked to do it quickly.

"When you're playing over the tight end, everything happens *right now* because the guy's right on top of you," says Peter Giunta, the Rams current defensive coordinator. "It happens instantaneously. Plus, you've got to be fairly strong to take a guy on right on the line of scrimmage. You've got to use your hands and play with good leverage."

As if that weren't enough of an adjustment, playing the complicated Carson system was unlike anything Mike had ever done on a football field. "That defense makes you a better all-around player, but it's a tough defense," Mike says. "It's going to make you do everything."

Including think. The system calls for players to adjust their pass coverage and defensive front based on the formation and the backfield of the opposing team. To do this, the defense has to wait for the opposing team to break the huddle and line up. This gives the defense no more than 10 seconds to recognize, react, and make the proper calls. It's like a quick, violent chess match. If you make the wrong calls and line up in the wrong position, it can be disastrous. And in the early going of that 1997 season, it was disastrous, especially for Mike and the Rams' other starting outside linebacker, Roman Phifer.

The Vermeil era opened with a preseason game in Minnesota. The Vikings' high-tech offense featured lots of shifts and motions, each one of which might require one of those split-second calls and adjustments by the Rams' defense. It was mass confusion. Even dropping off into the right area in pass coverage proved to be an ordeal.

"We were just clueless," Mike admits. "I was looking over at Roman: *'Okay, where are you dropping?'* And Roman was looking over at me like, *'I don't know where I'm dropping either.'* "

As the game progressed, they just kind of moved to the nearest open spot and hoped for the best. After the game, Bunting pulled Mike and Phifer aside. Mike remembers a conversation like this:

Bunting: "You guys didn't play very well."

Mike and Phifer: "We didn't know very much either."

Bunting (with a laugh): "I understand what you're saying. Whatever you lack in knowledge, make up in aggression. If you don't know what you're doing, just do it 100 miles an hour."

So for much of that 1997 season, the Rams outside linebackers didn't always know where they were going, but they got there quickly. Sometimes this helter-skelter approach actually confused opposing quarterbacks and offensive coordinators. But it also made the Rams more susceptible to the big play. The more polished and disciplined offenses were able to catch the Rams out of position and make them pay.

"It was like Game 3 or 4 of the regular season, and we were still swimming, trying to stay afloat," Mike remembers. "It was a little crazy."

Somehow, the Rams managed to start the season 2–2, narrowly missing a 3–1 start because of a heart-wrenching 15–12 loss to San

Francisco. Then the bottom fell out of the season. The Rams lost their next eight games. Five of those defeats were by eight points or less.

"It got so frustrating," Mike says. "I remember thinking, *'I'm back in my Mizzou days.'*"

The Rams did manage to win three of their final four contests, but their 5–11 record was one game worse than the 6–10 mark that had gotten Rich Brooks fired the year before.

"I knew the first year we were going to have problems because it was the first year of the program," Mike says. "It was almost like an expansion team if you think about it. We had all new players, a new coaching staff. And it was a coaching staff that none of us really knew."

A Feeling-Out Period

It took some time to get to know Vermeil. "When he first got there, there was a gap of 14 years since he last coached," Mike says. "So the only people you could talk to that had played for him were the coaches. And that's a strange question to ask a coach: 'What's Coach Vermeil like? Granted, you played for him. But you work for him now.' So you couldn't really get a fair judgment." (Rams assistant coaches John Bunting, Carl "Big Daddy" Hairston, and Wilbert Montgomery had all played for Vermeil in Philadelphia.)

"After you play for him, you can see why guys loved him," Mike says. "But the first year, no one could talk to him because no one knew *how* to talk to him. No one felt like they could approach him because they didn't really understand Coach Vermeil.

"And I think you could say the same thing for Coach Vermeil. Coach Vermeil did everything he could, but he didn't really know us because he hadn't coached in so long. He knew guys from watching them play because he covered games. But going in for a weekend to do a telecast and seeing somebody everyday from 9 to 5 [or longer] are two totally different things.

"We just had to learn each other. Defensively, it was even harder because Coach Vermeil was an offensive coach. He was never over there [in the defensive meetings]."

Getting used to Vermeil's emotions also took some doing. Long before the Rams led the league in victories, Vermeil led the football world in hugs, misty eyes, and downright tears. In fact, he frequently choked up when one of his former players or longtime coaching associates spoke to the Rams at a minicamp or training camp.

By the time the 1998 training camp rolled around, the Rams were getting used to this facet of Coach Vermeil. In fact, Mike and Roman

Phifer would kid each other about Vermeil's emotional tendencies:

Mike: "Roman, when you retire, is Coach Vermeil going to cry for you when he gives the speech?"

Phifer: "No, he'll probably cry for you."

"We had a little fun with it," Mike admits. "And eventually, he had a little fun with it. He would say, 'I'm an emotional guy. I'm going to cry every now and then.' He'd make fun of himself. But it got to a point where you knew he really cared about his players."

One event may best exemplify Vermeil's dedication to his staff and players, as well as his predisposition to becoming emotional. One day during the 1998 training camp, he became choked up when announcing to the team that Aaron Laing, at the time a third-string tight end, had been traded to Green Bay.

Small-World Department: Aaron Laing and Kevin Carter hosted a charity softball game during the off-season. When Laing was traded, Mike Jones agreed to step in to fill the void. The event is held during the Michael Jones Foundation Celebrity Weekend.

Vermeil's emotional investment in his team provided for some awkward moments when new players arrived. Take linebacker Eric Hill, a grizzled veteran of nine NFL seasons when he signed a free-agent contract with the Rams in 1998.

"Eric's sitting next to me in a meeting," Mike recalls. "Coach Vermeil's talking. He has a couple of his former players there, and he starts crying. Eric looks at me, and says, 'Man, what's wrong with him?'

"I tell Eric, 'That's Coach Vermeil. You better get used to it because that's going to be a weekly scenario right there. He's going to break down, sooner or later, once a week.' "

On the Brink

By the time training camp rolled around in 1998, most of the learning was over for the players. They knew the Rams' system and had a much better idea of what they were supposed to be doing from play to play, down to down. They also knew how to tell time.

"It started hitting everybody how long these practices were," Mike recalls. Just one week into camp, during a weekend of workouts with the Indianapolis Colts in Champaign, Illinois, Mike could tell the team was tired. "I mean, we were dragging," he says.

The team played fairly well in its preseason opener, a 20–13 loss to the defending Super

Bowl-champion Denver Broncos at the Trans World Dome. "And then we go back to training camp, and we're just banging again, just going at it," Mike says. "Then we go to San Diego for our next game, and it's a horrible trip."

First, there was the 1½-hour bus ride to Peoria from the Rams' training site in Macomb, Illinois. Then, there was a l-o-n-g flight to San Diego. "By the time the flight got up in the air, everybody on that plane was sleeping," Mike says. "You realized how tired everybody was just by looking around the plane.

"Usually, people are laughing and talking. It was almost like a day-care center at nap time. I mean, everybody was knocked out. We slept all the way to San Diego."

The plane arrived in sunny California the day before the game, leaving plenty of time to go to a mall, take a walk, get a bite to eat. "But guys stayed in their rooms and didn't do anything," Mike says. "They just rested."

Mike followed the lead of his teammates. "I just sat around the room," he says. "I went and got some McDonald's and went right back to the room."

The next night, things didn't go well against the Chargers. "We just stunk up the place," Mike recalls. "We blew coverages. We did a lot of bad stuff. We didn't play well at all."

The Rams lost 41–27. In the locker room after the game, several Rams were openly disgusted about the team's general state of fatigue. Making matters worse, the team was traveling back to Macomb for the final 2½ days of training camp instead of returning to St. Louis to continue preparations for the season at Rams Park. The team took a red-eye flight to Peoria following the game. In Peoria, it was back on the buses for the drive to Macomb. It was 9 A.M. the next morning when the players finally arrived at their dorm at Western Illinois University.

The Rams may have won their final two preseason games, against Dallas and Kansas City, but they didn't look sharp. "Instead of cutting practices down, we just kept on pouring it on and pouring it on," Mike says. "People were just falling off with injuries. It was more fatigue than anything."

At the start of the regular season, reporters were taken aback at the scene in the locker room during the daily interview period. On more than one occasion, the lights would be turned off and players would be sleeping by their locker stalls—in the middle of the day!

"People were tired, that was for sure," Mike says. "Instead of trying to get better, we were just trying to get through it."

And it showed during the regular season.

The team played with little energy or enthusiasm, particularly at the start of games. "Like practice, we were trying to pace ourselves," Mike says. "We tried to get through it."

Which was no way to win football games. In the season opener against New Orleans, the Rams fell behind by a shocking 24–0 late in the first half. They played much better in the second half, but they still fell short by a final score of 24–17.

"That was the way we played the whole season," Mike says. "It seemed like we'd start off slow and gradually get into it." In seven of the Rams' first 11 games that year, they trailed by at least 10 points in the first half. Not surprisingly, they lost eight of those 11 games.

Clearing the Air

Almost at the beginning of the 1998 regular season, the players decided to confront Vermeil on the issue of practice time and length of meetings. Preparations for such a confrontation began with a players-only meeting on September 14, 1998—the Monday after a 38–31 loss to Minnesota. (This wasn't the first time a Vermeil-coached team grumbled about practice times. His 1975 UCLA Rose Bowl team actually boycotted practice for one day over the same issue.)

"We had some guys come up front and say, 'We've got to change the practice schedule. They're too long,' " Mike recalls. "They said, 'We're starting off too slow, and the reason we're starting off slow is because that's the way we're practicing. And the reason why we're practicing like that is everyone's trying to get through practice.' "

After talking over their grievances, the players presented their concerns to Dick Vermeil. While recognizing their concern over practice times, Vermeil pointed out to the players that a more important goal was turning the program around. He reminded them that the Rams were still the losingest team in the '90s.

"There was a bunch of stuff that was said," Mike recalls.

Finally, Vermeil extended an olive branch: *"I understand you guys want to cut down on practices. We can do that. We can figure out a way where we can work together and get a better result."*

Vermeil made some changes in the team's practice schedule. But by the end of the year, practices were creeping back up to the three-hour mark, an occurrence that didn't go unnoticed by the players. So the results weren't exactly what the players were looking for, but something larger grew out of that September meeting.

"That was the first time the guys really started to understand Coach Vermeil," Mike says. "Even though it was a strange situation, that was the first time we were able to go to him and say, 'We want this changed, and we want that changed.' That might have been the turning point as far as relationships with players. That year, he started trusting a lot more players.

"Coach Vermeil and I always had a real good relationship because I always showed up and I always worked hard. That's all he ever wanted. He didn't have to push me. And that's what he wanted everybody to do. He didn't know if he got that from everybody.

"He signed some guys that didn't push themselves. He felt he got burned on a couple situations. So he still had his guard up. We didn't know him, so we had our guard up. But he started letting his guard down, and we started letting our guard down a little bit. Even though the season didn't go the way we wanted it to, a relationship was built right then and there.

"Now you can see why guys from Philadelphia come back and say they love Coach Vermeil and mean it sincerely. And you can see the way Coach Vermeil is because he's seen it work everywhere he's been. From high school, to college, to the NFL."

But it didn't look like the Vermeil system was

working in 1998, even if the seeds of a trusting player-coach relationship had been planted. The team regressed, finishing 4–12. This upset Mike immensely because he had firmly believed at the start of the season that the team was capable of winning at least eight games. But opposing teams seemed to pounce on every Rams mistake. It seemed like every Rams turnover took place deep in their own territory, giving the other team a short route to the end zone.

Rams Players Falter

In addition to learning a new system and a new staff, there seemed to be one off-the-field problem after another in the first two years of the Vermeil regime. When he wasn't encountering legal problems away from Rams Park, running back Lawrence Phillips was showing up late for meetings or missing them entirely. Quarterback Tony Banks brought his dog, Felony, to training camp one year. In 1998, he skipped the team flight home from Miami after a tough 14–0 loss and missed team meetings the following day. Rookie linebacker Leonard Little was involved in a drunken-driving traffic accident that claimed the life of a St. Louis County housewife. All this and more and the losses kept piling up.

If such off-the-field problems seemed to some to be indicative of the Rams in 1998, they were overlooking Mike Jones and many of his teammates who were concerned about making the plays and getting the job done. After a 20–17 loss to Arizona at the TWA Dome, a game in which the Rams let a late lead slip away, Mike stayed in the locker room long after the game. His teammates and even the media had long since cleared out. *"It just can't be so hard,"* Mike remembers thinking at the time as he gathered his thoughts to face his family.

Mike's brother Kevin remembers that September day well. As usual, the family had made the trek from Kansas City for the game. As usual, they wore their "KC Joneses" T-shirts in the stands. As usual, Kevin rode home with Mike in his 1991 Thunderbird. (Mike had bought the car in 1992 after his rookie season with the Raiders. More than six years later, he still drove it every day.)

"Mike's very frugal with his money," Kevin explains. "He doesn't spend it just blatantly. And that car, the windows wouldn't come down. The air conditioner didn't work. You couldn't open up one of the doors from the outside. And he's sitting in there, he was steaming because of the game, and it was hot."

Instead of trying to cheer Mike up, Kevin offered his kid brother some advice: *"Spend some money and get another car. This is ridiculous."*

(Mike finally gave in and bought some new wheels, but not until the following spring. "He gave the car to one of our sisters," Kevin says, "but it's still in his name. He's still not giving it up.")

Iron Mike

Who knows what else triggered in Mike's mind besides the desire for a new car, but Mike didn't give up. He continued to make the plays, despite how hard the road seemed to be. He registered career highs in tackles (106), sacks (three), and interceptions (two) in 1998. And despite the grueling training camp and all those long practices and meetings, Mike didn't miss a single defensive play for the entire 1998 season. The previous season, he had missed only two defensive plays out of 1,047. So in his first two seasons as a Ram, Mike had participated in an astounding 2,049 of 2,051 defensive plays. (In nine NFL seasons, Mike has played in 143 of 144 regular season games. Including post-season play, Mike has started 82 of his last 83 games as a Raider and a Ram.)

Mike's first missed play in 1997 was pure happenstance. With Atlanta about to snap the ball, Mike alertly noticed that the Rams had 12 men on the field. Rest assured, Mike was *supposed* to be out there. But rather than risk a penalty for too many men on the field, he sprinted off. "They ended up getting the first down anyway," Mike recalls.

A Frustrating Season Ends

Vermeil may have spent most of his time with the offense, but Mike's efforts in 1997 and 1998 didn't go unnoticed by the head coach. "He just kept getting better," Vermeil said. "I think sometimes Mike is so conscientious, he tries too hard to be perfect rather than just line up and play. But there aren't many linebackers who can stay in the ballgame and make the plays that he can make on every down."

But Vermeil didn't have enough playmakers in '97 or '98—particularly on offense, where Tony Banks wasn't working out at quarterback. The 1998 season concluded with a 38–19 loss in San Francisco. Several Rams players skipped a team meeting the next day, and to some, it looked like Vermeil was losing the team.

"It was just a totally frustrating year," Mike says. "After the season was over with, I was just shaking my head."

9

Christian Soldiers

Religious faith seems more prominent in football than in any other major professional sport in America. Where else do you see players from both teams gather on the field after a hard-fought contest, then drop to a knee in prayer?

Perhaps football players feel a step closer to God than their counterparts in baseball, basketball, and hockey. It seems that in no other sport does the specter of injury—serious, even life-threatening injury—loom on every play. Violence is a part of the game. Collisions take place on every snap.

Not since the 1991 Washington Redskins has there been a Super Bowl champion as openly religious as the 1999 St. Louis Rams. Sometimes the Rams have been so outspoken in their belief as to border on controversy. Take star wide receiver Isaac Bruce, for instance, describing an accident that totaled his car midway through the 1999 season. It was widely reported that Bruce confidently called on Jesus' name as his car was tumbling out of control into a ditch.

"I've been around some teams with spiritual guys," says Rams defensive tackle Ray Agnew, a veteran of 10 NFL seasons. "But this team is really spiritual. The thing that's great is some of our most looked-at athletes, Kurt [Warner] and Isaac, some of the most high-profile guys, are the most solid Christians. That means a lot because the young guys are looking up to these guys."

Count Mike Jones among those "solid Christians."

"He loves the Lord just like anyone of us," Agnew says. "He's very quiet. He doesn't run around swinging his Bible in everyone's face. But he's a solid guy as far as his faith in God."

Bringing the Team Together

Rams players don't openly force their beliefs on their teammates. But they're not shy about proclaiming their faith in Jesus Christ either. Over the course of a season, there are indications of this all over the locker room. Flyers remind players of a Bible study session at Warner's home. There's a Bible tucked into D'Marco Farr's locker. A small cross, fashioned from white adhesive tape, is seen stuck to the top of a locker stall. And Warner, of course, has openly used his fame as a forum to proclaim his faith in Jesus Christ as his Savior.

Dick Vermeil has coached football squads at every level, from high school, to junior college, to major college, to the NFL. So he's been exposed to all manner of Christians and varieties of beliefs in the locker room. But of his 1999 Rams, he says, "I thought this was a more sincere spiritual team. They all have different beliefs and different faiths. We've got Catholics; we've got Lutherans; we've got Baptists; we've got Presbyterians. Everybody. We've got 'em all.

"If it's a sincere feeling amongst the squad, it's just one more avenue that brings them together, maybe deeper than a lot of things do. I thought Ray Agnew and Mike Jones and Ernie Conwell and, of course, Kurt Warner helped generate those things. They'd get kids coming to Bible study who might be there because they didn't want to say no to Mike Jones or Ernie Conwell or Kurt Warner."

Vermeil adds, "I've always tried to make sure that we had leadership from a spiritual standpoint on our team. My first team [in Philadelphia], we had a monsignor that traveled with us the whole time. I learned a lot from him."

But when it comes to winning games on Sundays, Vermeil tries to make sure his players keep football and religion in perspective.

"God's not going to line up on one side of the line of scrimmage and help us win," Vermeil says. "Every once in a while you would find a kid so deeply involved in his faith that it was always the good Lord's will.

"Hey, it's *your* will. God isn't playing for you. He's providing you some depth of character and strength and some belief in yourself. But He wants you to do your job, regardless of whether it's football or whatever it may be."

Time with God

Perhaps sensing a special spiritual feeling among his 1999 squad, Vermeil asked Ray Agnew to say a pregame prayer before the Rams' September 26 game against Atlanta. Why Agnew?

"I have no idea," Agnew says. "I was kind of surprised, but I was glad. It's something that I love to do."

Prior to this, there had been no organized team prayer before games, but on this occasion the team gathered in the center of the locker room and knelt in prayer. Agnew then delivered a mini-sermon, lasting a couple of minutes. Agnew ended up saying a team prayer before and after every game.

"You pray for the spirit of winning, the spirit of playing hard. You pray for both teams to be safe—no injuries. But I never got down on my knees and said, 'God, we want to win 35–0.' I would never do that."

In addition to active participation in their home churches, many Rams players gathered to study the Bible. Warner's Bible study sessions usually took place on Wednesday nights during the season. Mike made a couple of these sessions but not many. The linebacker meetings usually ran longer than other positions on that day. But Mike and Leslie did attend a husband-and-wife session on Monday nights organized by Walt Enoch and Ricky Horton of the local chapter of the Fellowship of Christian Athletes. And on Friday mornings, there was a Bible study session for wives of players, wives of other Rams employees, and female employees at Rams Park.

"You have to stay in the Word," Leslie says.

Mike's Faith Walk

Mike grew up as a member of the Catholic church. He was an altar boy at St. Augustine's in Kansas City. "My mother and father always went to church," Mike says. "They made sure we went to church every Sunday. And they always tithed.

I didn't realize that until I got older. Every week, they gave their 10 percent. They always said that God always took care of them, so they give back." (Mike follows their faith example and tithes to the St. Louis City church he and his family attend—Transfiguration Lutheran.)

"My mother always made sure we did the right things," Mike says. "It was good because some of my friends didn't get that same guidance from their parents and people around them. When you're in the church all the time, you're not going to be able to get away with a whole bunch of stuff. That was good for us. We were around a lot of people that made sure we stayed on the straight and narrow."

Nonetheless, as he grew into adulthood, Mike's faith strayed from time to time. "I think that I struggled, just like everyone else struggled," Mike admits. "I try and make sure that when I get away from God that I try to get back to Him. Because if you don't, God will bring you back to Him. He will find a way to bring you back to Him."

In college, Mike wasn't a regular churchgoer during the school year. But that all changed once he returned home for the summer. "If you were staying in my mom's house, you were going to church," Mike says.

His faith has guided him through some tough

times, such as his breakup with Misty in 1991. Some of Mike's other personal lows may seem almost trivial to others, but they were very real to Mike at the time. Like his first varsity season at Southwest High when the school's proud football tradition suffered through a rare losing season. Or his junior year at Missouri when he temporarily lost his starting job to Jim White. "All those things made me stronger as a person," Mike says. "I had to have strong faith. I always had faith in God that He'd take care of me."

Mike's faith has fueled him through the good times as well. When it comes to his spirituality, Mike recognizes that God has given him many gifts—among them his saving faith in Jesus Christ, his tenacity, and his intellect, as well as his athletic ability. "He's blessed me with some talent to play, but a lot of people are blessed with talent that they don't use," Mike says. "That's one thing that I always talk to people about. 'God blessed you with talent. But your gift back to Him is using that talent.' "

On Super Bowl Sunday, as he locked in on the task at hand, namely, playing the most important football game of his life, Mike sat quietly at his locker with a headset on. Was he listening to:

A. Rap music.

B. Rhythm & blues.

C. Heavy metal.

D. Country & western.

The correct answer is "none of the above." Mike was listening to a gospel CD about David, of David and Goliath fame in 1 Samuel. "Basically, the CD is a tribute to David," Mike says. "Different songs and things like that."

Mike started listening to it around midseason, around the time the Rams played Detroit. He made it part of his weekly pregame routine. "It gets me ready to play," Mike says.

Young David, of course, was perhaps the ultimate biblical underdog. He was the youngest of seven sons and spent his early years as a shepherd. Later, God gave David the courage and strength to defeat the giant, Goliath, and eventually God made David king of the Israelites. Perhaps Mike sees a few parallels in the story of David and his own life. Mike, of course, was among the youngest in his family. He was very much the underdog at the start of his career. And he and the rest of the Rams perpetually seemed to be facing giants.

You could say Mike and his teammates approach football like David approached the giant Goliath. It's one way that they reconcile their Christianity with the fact that they play a violent sport. But it's also a matter of making the most of your God-given gifts, whatever they may be.

"I look at it like this: It's my job," Ray Agnew says. "My job is to hit the man in front of me into the quarterback and then hit the quarterback as hard as I can. My job is to play the game just as hard as anybody else. I can love the Lord and still hit a man as hard as I can. And I can tell him 'God bless you' after the play.

"The biggest misconception is that you'll lose your edge if you are a Christian. But I can say I've had more of an edge. I play the game to glorify God instead of me, and I play with all my might. I'm not going to back down from anybody. There's not a soft bone in me. There's nothing 'soft' about being a Christian."

And these are sentiments that Mike echoes when asked about the apparently odd mix of faith and football.

Faith and Family Life

Leslie, Mike, and their daughter, Ashley, attend Transfiguration Lutheran Church on 18th and Biddle streets near downtown St. Louis. It's a depressed neighborhood, situated near housing projects.

Leslie's mother, Melba, grew up in that area. Although her family eventually moved to the suburbs, they continued to worship at Transfiguration. And now Leslie and Mike attend as well. In fact, they were married at Transfiguration, and Ashley was baptized there.

"It's a real plus for the kids [of the congregation] to see someone like Mike in church," says the Reverend Frazier Odom. "They're quite amazed that Mike and Leslie, who have so many other things they could be doing, take so much time out to be in church and active at church."

Mike and Leslie's involvement at Transfiguration extends beyond attending weekly services. Leslie participates in the ladies' organization and is serving as the chair of the church's anniversary committee. They both participate in the church's summer Bible school program. And Mike also has served as coach for the Transfiguration basketball team, though he had to give up those duties because the Rams' 1999 postseason run corresponded with the start of the team's season.

"A lot of the kids that I was coaching at the church, they had never been in organized sports," Mike says. "And a lot of the kids weren't around a lot of males. So talking to the kids as a male adult, they weren't used to it.

"So I was hard on them. For the first year and a half, it took awhile for them to get used to me because they just weren't used to a male authority talking to them, and they hadn't had any structure as far as sports in their lives."

But the team got better. They weren't world-beaters, but they won their share of games.

Mike enjoys speaking to church groups, especially if kids are involved. At a recent gathering for the summer Bible school program, Reverend Odom relates that Mike was asked why he was in church so much. Didn't he have other things to do?

Reverend Odom says, "Mike told the group, 'The church is the most important part of my life. And if I'm going to be a role model, I need to lead by example, so I'm going to be in church.' "

As you might imagine, when Mike became a Ram in 1997, the members at Transfiguration became a lot more interested in Rams football. The church isn't located all that far from the Trans World Dome, so an early service at 9 A.M. was added during football season in case the faithful wanted to mix gridiron with Gospel on those Sundays when the Rams had a noon start.

Mike usually goes to the team chapel service on game days, unless the Rams are playing a late game. If that's the case, he drops by Transfiguration, sometimes bringing cornerback Todd Lyght or another teammate with him to hear Pastor Frazier Odom's sermon. Pastor

Odom is known in his congregation and community for his solid preaching—calling people to recognize their sins against God's Law, pointing them to the forgiveness Jesus won on the cross, and celebrating the hope of the resurrection that comes through faith in Jesus Christ. Pastor Odom shares the victory of the cross with his flock and with his community.

"He's a fireball," Mike says admiringly of Rev. Odom. "For some reason, I always picture Pastor Odom as an old David."

Although Mike is not the most outspoken member of the Rams when it comes to his beliefs, he is always willing to point people to the real power in his life. And Reverend Odom has seen a real change in Mike over the years.

"The more Mike shares his faith with others, the more comfortable he becomes," Reverend Odom explains. "He's gotten quicker and more at ease with his responses as he continues to answer questions about his faith in Jesus Christ."

10

A Super Season

The empty seats at the Trans World Dome toward the end of the 1998 season spoke volumes. Technically speaking, every game was a sellout, yet there were 15,000 no-shows—or unused tickets—in each of the final three home contests in 1998.

Four years after the move from Los Angeles, the honeymoon was over for the Rams in St. Louis. The team had gotten progressively worse since the move, slipping from 7–9 in 1995, to 6–10 in 1996, to 5–11 in 1997, and to 4–12 in 1998.

At this rate, or so the running joke went, the Rams were on target for an 0–16 finish in 2002. Something had to be done. And everyone in the Rams' hierarchy knew it—from owners Georgia Frontiere and Stan Kroenke, to president John Shaw, to executive vice president Jay Zygmunt, to vice president of player personnel Charley Armey.

At a summit meeting in Los Angeles in early January, Shaw impressed on Vermeil a sense of urgency about the 1999 campaign and a need for changes. The shakeup began by re-shuffling the coaching staff. Most notable was the ouster of Jerry Rhome as offensive coordinator and the hiring of Mike Martz—at the time quarterbacks coach in Washington—as his replacement.

Next, the Rams attacked free agency as never before. "Every year, it seemed like we moved a little slow in free agency," Mike recalls. "It was like we were a step slow. In '99, we stepped up. We had everything lined up and got super-aggressive, knowing we had to do something."

Boy, did they. Within the first few days of free agency, the Rams signed quarterback Trent Green (from Washington) and offensive guard Adam Timmerman (from Green Bay) to big-money contracts. Between the two players, the Rams were investing a potential $35.5 million. Then just before the draft, the Rams acquired Pro Bowl running back Marshall Faulk in a trade with Indianapolis. The price was unbelievably cheap: only a second-round and a fifth-round draft pick. It was like paying ground chuck prices for filet mignon.

"My first reaction was: *Something's not right,*" Mike says. "You don't trade a second and a fifth for Marshall Faulk. I don't care what anybody says. I just couldn't see it. I didn't understand that move from Indianapolis' standpoint."

But Mike loved it from the Rams' standpoint. "I was very excited," Mike says. "I thought everything was falling into place."

The Rams had spent a ton of money in the off-season to shore up the roster. They had given the offense a dramatic facelift, including drafting wide receiver Torry Holt of North Carolina State with their first-round pick. But if none of this worked, ... well, Vermeil would be fired. Plain and simple. In fact, Shaw told confidants during the 1999 preseason that the "magic" number for Vermeil was 3. If the Rams' won-loss record fell three games below the .500 mark early in the season—say 0–3 or 1–4—Vermeil would be fired immediately. Shaw even had offensive line coach Jim Hanifan targeted as interim head coach. Of course, it never got to that. But that's how thin the margin of error was for Vermeil and the Rams entering the 1999 campaign.

"I knew he had to win," Mike says. "We hadn't gotten better, and we had been losing. You can't have both of those things. If we were getting better as a team—if we'd won five games his first year and then won seven—then you'd have something to build on."

But that hadn't been the case. Vermeil's Rams had regressed. "And the morale of the team was down," Mike says. "There was a bunch of stuff that was going on. It was almost like he was losing the team. So if things didn't work out, Coach Vermeil was in some trouble."

Captain Mike

As early as the spring 1999 minicamps, the offense was humming under Martz and Green. Suddenly, the talk by Vermeil wasn't about getting better—it was about making the playoffs.

Also early in training camp, Mike suffered a rare injury, twisting his knee during a joint practice session with the Indianapolis Colts in Champaign, Illinois. It wasn't a serious injury, but it was enough to sideline him for a couple of weeks.

Mike was reduced to spectator's status for a Saturday scrimmage against the Colts, which would end a three-day stay in Champaign. The Rams looked very sharp in the scrimmage. When Mike walked into the locker room after the game, several teammates approached him.

Teammates: "Mike, you've got to talk to Coach Vermeil."

Mike: "Why do I have to talk to Coach Vermeil?"

Teammates: "See if we can get tomorrow off."

So Mike approached Vermeil.

Mike: "Coach, why don't you let us have tomorrow off and not have meetings. Let us come back Monday."

Vermeil: "I don't think I'll be able to do that, Mike."

Vermeil started to walk away. But after a couple of steps, he stopped, looked at Mike, and smiled. Then he said: *"They know who to send when they want something, don't they?"* (The more Vermeil got to know Mike, the harder he found it to say no to Mike. And the players knew this.)

Vermeil gave the Rams the rest of the weekend off. After that, Mike's teammates started calling him "Mike Vermeil," as if he were the teacher's pet. But this wasn't the first time the players sent Mike as an emissary to Vermeil. And it wouldn't be the last.

"Every time there was any kind of a problem—the squad or anyone had a complaint—he'd come knocking on my office door and express his opinion," Vermeil says. "He would be the spokesperson. The players knew I had tremendous respect for him and cared for him. The chances of getting me to think about it more seriously were better when he brought in the message."

His teammates also had tremendous respect for Mike, naming him a team captain for the 1998 and 1999 seasons.

"He's a pretty quiet individual," linebacker London Fletcher says. "If you look at Mike Jones, he's more of a leader by example. When I was a rookie in 1998 and just trying to see where I fit in as a player in the National Football League, I remember watching him, watching how his approach was to the game."

What did Fletcher see? "Just his attitude on the field," Fletcher says. "He never missed a practice. He tries to make sure he's prepared for the game. He'd be the linebacker who stayed watching film after all the other linebackers had gone home."

Fletcher confesses, with a laugh: "I stole some of his techniques. I don't let him know that. But I've definitely learned a lot from him by watching him. It's made me a better football player."

And Fletcher has learned by watching Mike off the field as well. "He's a guy who is involved in a lot of different things," Fletcher says. "To be involved with as many things as he's involved in, you have to be a very prepared individual and very organized.

"He cares about people. That's why he does so many things for the kids with the free football camps. He does it because he cares."

Mike's low-key style of leadership obviously works because it has been recognized by his coaches and peers at every level of football. He was a team captain at Southwest High, at the University of Missouri, with Sacramento of the World League, and now with the Rams. This is a pattern, not a fluke.

"Leadership is not a process," Vermeil says. "It's a relationship. It's a relationship developed by respect and communication. He has that ability. People will follow him. People will listen to him."

"I think I relate well to everybody, whether they're white guys or black guys, young guys or old guys," Mike admits. "I want the guys I play with to feel they can trust me and that we're a family."

Sometimes being a leader means letting others do the talking.

"London is a talker," Mike says. "So sometimes I just sit back in the huddle and listen to London. London might be going off: *'We got to do this and that!'* Kevin (Carter) and I just look at each other: *'Yeah! That's what we've got to do.'* "

Easy Does It

Sometimes being a leader means doing the talking. Before the start of the 1999 training camp, Mike got some points across to his teammates.

Fellas, we can't have the distractions we had last year. Last year, we started worrying about everything other than football. We were worrying about how long practices were instead of worrying about getting better. We've got to worry about getting better and winning. If we're doing that, and we're not winning because the system's not working, then we've got to go in and tell Coach Vermeil.

But it never got to that. There were no near revolts, no player-coach confrontations. In one of the biggest upsets of the season, Vermeil changed the team's training camp routine. Make no mistake, Camp Vermeil wasn't suddenly transformed into the Club Med. But practice and meeting times were cut back noticeably. The number of practices in full pads was reduced dramatically. The Rams got more days off or afternoons off and fewer meetings.

"Everyone said John Shaw and Jay Zygmunt told Coach Vermeil he had to change his ways and the way he coached," Mike says. "And that might have had a little bit to do with it. But I think it was more that he trusted his players.

"Coach Vermeil had gotten players that he trusted, that would buy into what he wanted to do. So he trusted everybody and trusted that we would work smart and hard."

And that's what happened. Team spirit was high when the Rams broke camp. In stark contrast to the 1998 season, the players were fresh, enthusiastic, and upbeat when they returned to St. Louis. Trent Green, the new quarterback, looked good on the practice field. Very good.

Meanwhile, Mike was still sidelined by his knee injury when the Rams opened preseason play against his old team, the Oakland Raiders.

"I saw Al Davis before the game," Mike says. "I'm on the sideline in street clothes, and we're warming up on their side of the field. So as our linebackers are doing their drills, Al and I are talking and laughing, talking about the Raiders like I'm still on the team."

They spoke for a good 15 minutes. The conversation was free and easy. It was almost as if Mike had never left. *"Mike, I wish I could have kept you,"* Davis said. Davis also said one of his scouts had talked him into thinking that Mike Morton was ready to replace Mike in the starting lineup.

As if to prove his point, Davis approached

Mike after the game. The scout in question was standing next to Davis. *"Tell him what I told you. Tell him what I told you,"* Davis said to the scout.

"You were right, Al," the scout replied. *"You told me you wanted to keep Mike. It was my fault that Mike didn't come back."*

Then the scout and Al Davis walked away.

"I loved playing for the Raiders," Mike says. "The mystique of playing for the Raiders— unless you've played for them, there's nothing like it. Putting on that helmet, putting on that jersey. I didn't realize until I got there what it was like. I have nothing but good things to say about Al."

The feeling is mutual. In fact, the mere sight of Mike brings out a little Vermeil in Davis. "Every time we see each other, we hug because I'm personally fond of him," Davis says. "He fits everything you'd want in a person and a player, let's be honest about it. He wore the Silver & Black with poise and pride."

Green Goes Down

Green simply couldn't miss during the pre-season. Of his 32 passes in exhibition play, 28 were complete. Two of the four misses were dropped passes. On the night of August 28 at the Trans World Dome, Green completed a 12-yard pass late in the second quarter against San

Diego. He was an astounding 11 for 11 at this point in the game.

But before that pass reached wide receiver Tony Small, blitzing Chargers safety Rodney Harrison came crashing into the back of Green's left knee. Green crumpled to the turf as if shot. Just like that, his season was over. He would need reconstructive knee surgery.

To say the Rams were angered by Harrison's hit—which most observers considered a "cheap shot"—would be an understatement. "Everybody was so mad on the sidelines, there was a possibility that we were going to run on the field and get that guy," Mike says. "That's how upset everybody was when we saw Trent go down."

Wide receiver Isaac Bruce slammed his helmet to the turf in disgust. Rams players started yelling at Harrison. Mike had words with Chargers linebacker Eric Hill, a former Ram.

Mike: "That wasn't right, what your guy did."

Hill: "I don't know what to tell you, Mike."

One thing was for certain: Any optimism about the Rams' prospects in 1999 vanished as Green was carted off the field. The team would be lucky to win six games without him—or so went the conventional wisdom—especially since the number 2 quarterback was an obscure player named Kurt Warner.

Warner barely made the team as third-string quarterback in 1998. He had thrown only 11 regular-season passes as an NFL player. Now he was being counted on to lead the Rams out of the wilderness.

How obscure was Warner? Well, he had trouble even getting into the weekly pickup basketball games Mike attended at a local high school during the off-season. Keep in mind, the vast majority of participants were "civilians," not NFL football players like Mike and Warner. But when participants picked sides for the five-on-five full-court games, they'd skip Kurt. "He just didn't get picked," Mike says. "I guess they didn't think he could play."

Warner was relegated to the sidelines with the other scrubs and had to wait his turn. Eventually, Warner got his turn and played very well. After all, he had been a high school hoops star growing up in Iowa. Not that anyone knew who he was on those Fridays at Parkway North High in suburban St. Louis.

"After we got done playing basketball, the other guys were like, 'Who is that guy?' " Mike recalls. " 'He's our backup quarterback,' I told them."

But that all changed with Green's injury. The day after the San Diego game, Vermeil rallied the troops around Warner. *"Kurt Warner's our quarterback,"* Vermeil told the squad. *"He's got a lot of responsibility, but we're going to ride it out. We're not going to bring anybody else in to start."*

Vermeil then turned toward Warner and said: *"This is your team."* Roughly 70 sets of eyes turned toward Warner—the entire roster and coaching staff.

"Everybody's looking at Kurt," Mike says. "And everybody's thinking, *'Is he excited? Is he scared?'* "

Who could tell? "Kurt had the same look on his face," Mike recalls. "He was just nodding his head. You couldn't get a feel if he was nervous or what."

Warner didn't look nervous in the preseason finale against Detroit—his first starting assignment as an NFL quarterback. He led the Rams on three scoring drives in the first half—two touchdowns and a field goal—before the reserves took over.

But Mike got nervous when he saw Warner—who's not known for his mobility—scrambling down the field on a broken play with several Lions in pursuit. The Rams already had one injured quarterback. They didn't need two. As Warner reached the sidelines after that series, he received a lecture from Mike. *"Kurt, the next time you run like that—I'm going to tackle you."*

Off and Running

The Rams exhaled after the Detroit game. Warner hadn't done anything spectacular, but he had been efficient, mistake-free, and seemed cool in the pocket. Spirits were lifted. But could he play like this once the regular season started? The answer, of course, was a resounding yes!

In season-opening victories over Baltimore, Atlanta, and Cincinnati, the Rams outscored the opposition by a combined 100–27. The Atlanta game was key. Yes, the Falcons were without star running back Jamal Anderson—lost for the season a week earlier with a knee injury. But they remained the defending NFC champions until proven otherwise.

Atlanta had won four straight over the Rams since Mike came to St. Louis in 1997, and the St. Louis defense had played poorly in all four contests. *"The Atlanta game is going to be telltale for our season,"* Mike said before the game. *"Because they've been pounding us every time."*

But not this time. With Warner throwing three touchdown passes, the Rams raced to a 28–0 halftime lead before coasting in with a 35–7 victory in Game 2 of the young season.

After a 38–10 victory over Cincinnati, Warner had thrown nine TDs with only two interceptions in three games. The following week, Mike got a call from one of the off-season basketball regulars at Parkway North.

"Is that the same Kurt Warner who used to play basketball with us?" the caller asked. *"The guy we wouldn't pick?"*

"The exact same one," Mike replied.

The acid test had yet to come—the mighty San Francisco 49ers. They had won 17 straight against the Rams, the third-longest winning streak in a team vs. team series in NFL history. Sure, the 49ers were coming to the TWA Dome without star quarterback Steve Young and star running back Garrison Hearst. But injuries never seemed to matter. The 49ers always found a way to beat the Rams. Besides, the 49ers were 3–1 without Young and Hearst and were coming off a victory over Tennessee.

Mike experienced an unusual sensation on the practice field that Friday, less than 48 hours before kickoff. "We went through a flawless practice," Mike says. "Guys were flying around, and no one's saying anything. It's not like we were uptight; everyone was just completely focused on what they had to do. You could just look at all the guys and know, *'We're about to beat these guys.'*

"Then we go into the game, and I don't think the 49ers know what hit them."

Isaac Bruce caught four touchdown passes. Mike had his first interception of the season plus seven tackles. After sprinting to a 21–3 first-quarter lead, the Rams snapped the long losing streak with a resounding 42–20 victory.

After the game, 49ers general manager Bill Walsh came into the Rams' interview room just as Vermeil was finishing his postgame news conference. Walsh gave Vermeil—one of his oldest and dearest friends—a big hug. In a stage whisper heard by most of the assembled press, Walsh said, *"You're going all the way, baby."*

Vermeil, slightly taken aback, replied, *"Don't say that."*

Bumps in the Road

So the Rams were 4–0 and rolling. This once-hapless team had reached the point at which they expected to win each game. Following a second victory over Atlanta, and a 34–3 triumph over the expansion Cleveland Browns, the Rams took a spiffy 6–0 record to Nashville for an October 31 game with the 5–1 Tennessee Titans.

The rest of the league had begun to take notice of the upstart Rams. And so had the nation's press. With reporters from all over the country crammed into the Adelphia Coliseum press box, the Rams finally had a chance to strut their stuff before a national audience.

They promptly fell victim to acute stage fright. Before you could say "gotta go to work"—the Rams' unofficial team slogan—the Titans had taken a 21–0 first-quarter lead.

"We were tight," Mike says. "I shouldn't say we were tight. We were just trying to do too much. Instead of a guy doing his job, he was trying to do his job and somebody else's job."

As a result, they didn't get the job done. But instead of wilting, they rallied. Only a missed 38-yard field goal by Jeff Wilkins with 7 seconds to play prevented the game from going into overtime. The Titans escaped with a 24–21 victory. The Rams were unbeaten no more, but they headed back to St. Louis with the knowledge that they had been in position to win despite a terrible start.

"We knew as badly as we played, we had played them to a standstill on their field," Mike says. "I was telling everybody after that game: 'If we're on a neutral field, we're going to beat them. Because we're not going to make the same mistakes we made this time.' "

It was a nice thought. But the only way the teams would meet again was in the Super Bowl. And we all knew that would never happen. Right?

The Rams' defensive front seven didn't play well against the Titans, Mike included. He got caught out of position on a screen pass to Eddie George, and the Titans running back scored Tennessee's second touchdown on the play. Rams linebackers coach John Bunting and defensive line coach Carl Hairston challenged their units to do better the next week in Detroit.

Playing against former Rams running back Greg Hill, who was shipped to the Lions in a preseason trade, the Rams' front seven got after it in the Silverdome. A popular player in St. Louis, Hill visited the Rams' team hotel the night before the game. He visited with several former teammates, Mike included. All pleasantries ended on game day, though.

"We stuffed him on his first couple runs, and Greg got frustrated," Mike says. "It got to a point where Greg was getting mad at his offensive line. And we weren't even saying anything to him. We'd make the tackle. We'd hop up, help Greg up." And then tackle him again.

Defensively, the game plan went exactly as planned. The Rams wanted to stop the run and force Detroit to try to beat them with their passing game. Well, they stopped the run all right. Hill finished with a mere three yards on 11 carries. But Lions quarterbacks Charlie Batch and Gus Frerotte combined for 357 yards passing and three TD passes. The Lions rallied for a 31–27 victory, scoring the game-winning touchdown pass with 28 seconds to play.

So much for that strategy of thinking the Lions couldn't beat them with the pass. "How wrong we were on that one," Mike says.

The air of invincibility was gone. The Rams were a mortal 6–2. With Atlanta and San Francisco both having fallen on hard times, none of those six victories had come over teams that were playoff contenders. Maybe appearances *were* deceiving. Maybe the Rams weren't an elite team after all.

Stone Fingers

Back home after those wrenching road losses, the offense came out sluggish November 14 against Carolina. But a little bit of espionage by Mike helped the Rams return to their winning ways.

Late in the second quarter, Carolina's Pro Bowl tight end Wesley Walls ran a quick sideline pattern. Mike's responsibility on the play was to cover fullback William Floyd, who was coming out of the Panthers' backfield. Walls was wide open on the play, but Carolina quarterback Steve Beuerlein threw the ball elsewhere.

As Walls jogged back to the huddle, he told Beuerlein: *"You know that play is open."*

Beuerlein nodded and replied: *"We're going to come back to that play."*

Neither Beuerlein nor Walls knew it at the time, but Mike was eavesdropping on this conversation. "You'd be amazed how much you can hear on the field if you listen," Mike says. (Mike also has become an accomplished on-the-field lip reader.)

Early in the third quarter, Beuerlein was true to his word. Carolina ran the same pattern. Mike covered Floyd out in the flat. But this time, as Beuerlein threw the ball to Walls, Mike peeled off Floyd and sprinted over to Walls. With Walls dragging Rams safety Billy Jenkins for extra yardage, Mike pounced on the tight end from behind and stripped the ball loose.

Mike was near the sideline, and the ball took two bounces before he grabbed it and raced 37 yards for a victory-clinching touchdown in a 35–10 triumph. It was the first of three touchdowns scored by Mike in the 1999 season, a league-leading total for a defensive player.

The next week in San Francisco, Mike struck again. With the Rams nursing a 13–7 lead early in the third quarter, Mike grabbed a pass tipped by teammate D'Marco Farr and raced 44 yards for a touchdown in what became a 23–7 Rams victory. This time, Mike tried to celebrate by doing the team's Bob & Weave touchdown dance. It was an underwhelming performance. Just ask London Fletcher.

"His Bob & Weave was like the worst," Fletcher says. "He looked like the Tin Man."

Realizing his rhythmic limitations, Mike asked Fletcher to teach him the "Sugarfoot." That was the name Fletcher had given to his own high-stepping, prancing dance—a routine performed after making a big tackle or a sack. Alas, Mike's request was rejected.

"After I saw him do the Bob & Weave, I didn't want him tearing down my dance," Fletcher says, chuckling.

That wasn't the only ribbing Mike would take in the regular season. Despite those interceptions and defensive touchdowns, D'Marco Farr let it be known that Mike had a new nickname in the locker room: "Hands of Stone Jones." It seems Mike had earned the nickname by dropping more than his share of interceptions on the practice field. After watching his running style on his interception returns, teammates also found it hard to believe that Mike had been a college running back.

"I want to see the game film," Fletcher cackled at the time.

It was all in good fun. The Rams were rolling toward the postseason with Mike racking up one big play after another. The playoffs had become a foregone conclusion after that November 21 victory in San Francisco, but the Rams remained highly motivated. Every week, they were playing for a meaningful goal:

- Game 11 vs. New Orleans: The Rams clinch their first winning season since 1989 with a 43–12 triumph.

- Game 12 vs. Carolina: The Rams clinch the NFC West title and their first playoff berth since 1989 with a 34–21 victory.

- Game 13 vs. New Orleans: The Rams complete NFC West play with a perfect 8–0 record by defeating the Saints 30–14.

- Game 14 vs. the New York Giants: Aided by Mike's third TD of the season—a 22-yard interception return—the Rams clinch a first-round bye plus home-field advantage throughout the NFC playoffs with a 31–10 victory.

- Game 15 vs. Chicago: A 34–12 rout completes a perfect home season (8–0).

Only in Game 16, the regular-season finale in Philadelphia, did the Rams have absolutely nothing to play for. With Dick Vermeil resting his regulars, the Rams lost 38–31 at Veterans Stadium. Despite the loss, the Rams were about to make St. Louis football history. Never before had a St. Louis professional football team played a home playoff game—until now.

The Road to Atlanta

The Minnesota Vikings provided the opposition for the Rams' playoff opener. In the days leading up to the game, the story line centered around the Vikings' high-octane offense of Randy Moss, Cris Carter, Robert Smith, and quarterback Jeff George. Unlike the Rams, this was an experienced, playoff-savvy team. And despite all the points scored by the Rams' pinball offense, the larger question seemed to be: *Could the Rams' defense contain Minnesota?*

There also remained a degree of skepticism concerning the Rams. In fashioning a 13–3 regular-season record, not one victory came against a playoff team. In fact, not one victory came against a team that finished the season with a winning record.

In the opening minutes of play, the crowd was so loud at the TWA Dome that the Rams couldn't hear London Fletcher make the defensive calls in their own huddle.

"He would tell like two of us, and we would relay the message around the huddle," Mike says.

There was no doubt about it. Rams fans were pumped up like never before. And so were the Rams. "For a lot of guys, it was their first playoff game," Mike says. "It was the first home playoff game in the history of St. Louis.

There was just so much going on that it was easy to get caught up in the hype of the game. But sooner or later, you knew you had to play football."

The Vikings did their best to knock the Rams back to reality, taking a 17–14 lead at halftime. Maybe the Rams were overrated. Maybe the less-than-stellar opposition they had faced during the regular season would finally catch up with them.

On defense, the Rams were missing tackles, blowing assignments, and generally not playing smart. It was an uncharacteristic performance. But there was no yelling, no screaming, no furniture tossing in the locker room at halftime. The message was surprisingly simple.

"The coaches told us we just needed to play football and not get caught up in the emotions of the game," Mike says. "We needed to play like we'd always played, and then we'd be fine."

Just like that, the Rams calmed down and went about their business in dramatic fashion. The avalanche began with a 95-yard kickoff return for a score by Tony Horne to start the third quarter. In the next 1½ quarters, the Rams would outscore Minnesota 35–0. Over that same span, the Vikings' offense was stopped dead in its tracks to the tune of *minus* 8 yards.

"Jeff George started getting hit, and that was our whole game," Mike recalls. "If we could get after him and hit him a couple of times, we knew he'd get flustered."

It was an astounding display of domination by St. Louis across the board. Offense. Defense. Special teams. When tight end Roland Williams caught a touchdown pass midway through the fourth quarter, the Rams had a 49–17 lead. Dick Vermeil sent in the junior varsity, and the Vikings scored three late cosmetic TDs in a 49–37 Rams victory.

The defeat of Minnesota meant that Tampa Bay was the only hurdle remaining between the Rams and a trip to Super Bowl XXXIV in Atlanta's Georgia Dome. With a conservative, ground-oriented offense, and a quick, aggressive defense, the Buccaneers presented an entirely different challenge than Minnesota.

The Rams weren't going to score 49 points against the Bucs, and everyone at Rams Park knew it. But the Rams also knew Tampa Bay wouldn't score many points either. "If we got up on them, we knew Tampa Bay didn't play well from behind," Mike says. "All during the week we were thinking we matched up well defensively against them. It would be hard for them to score on us. And it was. They had six points."

But midway through the fourth quarter, it

looked like six points would be enough. The Bucs were leading by a baseball-like score of 6–5. Eighteen games into a record-setting season and the Rams' offense had finally met its match. Mike was getting concerned, as was everyone else in the TWA Dome with a rooting interest in the Rams.

"I knew we would come to a game sometime in the season where the defense would have to win a game," Mike says. "And it came down to the NFC championship."

With the clock ticking away, it was time for Captain Mike to challenge his teammates in the huddle. *"Guys, we've got 8 minutes left in this season. We've got to make a play."*

Just a couple of plays later, Mike thought it would be him. Covering Tampa Bay running back Warrick Dunn out of the backfield, Mike watched as Bucs quarterback Shaun King threw the football *right at him.*

"I'm thinking, *I've got an interception,*" Mike says. "I had a bead on the ball; I was right there. My hands were up to catch the ball. And all of a sudden, I see a flash come by me."

The flash was rookie cornerback Dre' Bly. Bly intercepted the pass and returned it to the Tampa Bay 47-yard line with 8:01 to play. The Bucs' defense gave ground grudgingly. Six plays and nearly 3½ minutes later, the Rams had advanced the ball only 17 yards.

On third and 4, Kurt Warner heaved a deep ball down the left sidelines. Mike and his defensive teammates were standing and shouting by the Rams' bench: *"There's 'Clutch'! He's going to make the play for us."*

"Clutch" being veteran wide receiver Ricky Proehl. With Tampa Bay defender Brian Kelly grabbing him, with the ball almost sliding off his hip, with the out-of-bounds line oh-so-close, "Clutch" made the grab. It was a 30-yard TD grab with 4:44 to play.

The dome erupted. But there was more work to be done. Tampa Bay drove from its own 23 to the Rams' 22 with 1:25 to play. Then came the play that has Rams defensive coordinator Peter Giunta still raving months after the fact.

On first and 10 from the St. Louis 22, defensive end Grant Wistrom sacked King for a 13-yard loss. Give Wistrom his due; it was a huge sack. But the guy who made the play, Giunta says, was Mike Jones.

On the play, the Rams sent Mike and London Fletcher up the middle on a blitz. Dunn, who stayed in the backfield to protect King, barely got over in time to get a piece of Mike. "But Mike throws himself at the quarterback," Giunta says, going over game film in mid-May. "Look at Mike keep going! He's rolling after King, and then Grant comes off the edge and makes the big sack. That is a huge pressure by Mike. It set up the rest of the game."

Despite getting knocked off his feet, Mike had continued to go after King and had gotten a hand on him. Although King was able to get away, in doing so, he gave Wistrom enough time to tackle him.

The Bucs never got out of that second-and-23 hole, and the Rams eked out an 11–6 victory. Amazingly, those former NFL sadsacks—the St. Louis Rams—were Super Bowl-bound. They were taking Georgia to Georgia.

The Halas Trophy, emblematic of the NFC championship, was presented to the Rams. Players took a victory lap around the dome, sharing the moment with their delirious fans. As a native Missourian, Mike thought about how special the moment was for St. Louis. As a nine-year NFL veteran, he thought about how special the moment was for players like Proehl and Todd Lyght and Keith Lyle, all of whom had never even been in a playoff game until the 1999 season. Now they were going to the Super Bowl. All of them.

"It was something special," Mike recalls. "I'm on the sidelines, and I'm just looking at everybody. There were guys getting emotional and crying."

Not Mike.

"We've got one more game to go, fellas," Mike told his teammates. *"We've got one more thing to do before we can start crying."*

11

The Game and The Tackle

There was absolutely no time for the Rams to celebrate the narrow escape against Tampa Bay. Unlike most Super Bowl seasons, only one week instead of two separated the conference championship games and Super Bowl XXXIV. Mike Jones and the Rams were on a plane for Atlanta less than 24 hours after defeating the Bucs.

For friends and relatives attending the big game, there were ticket, travel, and hotel concerns. Mike footed the bill for 13 tickets—the maximum available for purchase per player. He also paid for a charter bus to take more than 40 relatives to Atlanta. (Most would not actually attend the game.)

At least Mike's family helped to make the travel arrangements and he didn't have practice on Tuesday. Other than media day responsibilities, the players spent Tuesday settling into their hotel rooms in Atlanta. The Rams' coaching staff, however, didn't have it so easy.

Except for Dick Vermeil, the staff stayed in St. Louis on Monday and most of Tuesday, working into the wee hours on the game plan for the AFC Champion Tennessee Titans. Rams players and coaches didn't get together on the practice field in Atlanta until Wednesday. It wasn't a joyous reunion.

"The first day, I think, it was a combination of the coaches not having any sleep and the players being a little giddy about being in a Super Bowl," Mike says. Which made for a volatile combination. "The first practice wasn't good, but it was blown out of proportion, I think, by the coaches because everyone was out there yelling and screaming."

The constant yapping of special teams coach Frank "Crash" Gansz was a given. At almost every practice throughout the year, Gansz barked nonstop at the defense, talking to no one in particular. The players were used to this and could cope with it. Gansz' chatter had become a form of rapid-fire Muzak, blending into the scene like background music.

But on Super Bowl Wednesday, Gansz was merely one voice in a chorus. "Coach Vermeil was putting his part in; Peter [Giunta] was putting his part in; J.B. [John Bunting] was having his say; and you had Brownie [secondary coach Steve Brown]," Mike says. "Before you knew it, it was chaos out there because everybody was yelling and screaming."

On a defense that needs to make a lot of calls and checks at the line of scrimmage, the Rams couldn't hear themselves think. "So I'm out there thinking, *'Man. Everybody just needs to calm down,'* " Mike recalls.

But the madness continued. Finally, defensive end Kevin Carter had enough. When you think of team leaders on the Rams, Carter's name normally doesn't come up. But when he speaks, almost everyone listens. He didn't speak at this practice. He shouted. *"Shuuut uppp!"*

"Everybody just kind of looked at him," Mike recalls. "And they shut up."

Even the coaches.

The Thursday practice went much better. After Friday's workout, part-owner Stan Kroenke addressed the team. "He got a little emotional," Mike says. Kroenke is an amiable sort, but this seemed out of character.

"I know that's what everyone was saying," Mike says. "He got a little teary-eyed. He said he was so proud of what we'd accomplished."

Saturday's walk-through session at the Georgia Dome was canceled because of bad weather. Atlanta had reacted to an ice storm as if it were the second coming of the Ice Age. The town had practically shut down. Just like that, the practice week was over. There was nothing left to do but play the game.

Well, almost nothing. Because of the ice storm, Tennessee place-kicker Al Del Greco was unavailable to tape a cat food commercial with Rams counterpart Jeff Wilkins at the Rams' hotel. A last-minute replacement was needed on Saturday. Guess who?

With the TV cameras rolling, Mike and Wilkins proceeded to sing that catchy feline jingle: *"Meow, meow, meow, meow ... meow, meow, meow, meow ... meow, meow, meow, meow..."*

Turns out that was about the most Mike had to say all week. "Michael was more reserved than he normally is before a game," says his wife, Leslie. "He wasn't really talkative." It was as if Mike were trying to cut down on all outside interference, which Leslie could understand. "This was the biggest game of his career," she says.

Leslie flew down Thursday from St. Louis with a travel party that included her mother and father, Ashley, and Mike's mom, Mary Jo. (Mike's dad, Leroy Sr., doesn't like to fly.) Mike spent Thursday night with Leslie and Ashley at a nearby hotel before spending Friday and Saturday night at the team hotel.

Meanwhile, the "KC Joneses"—Mike's brothers, sisters, nieces, nephews, and cousins—were motoring to Georgia from Kansas City on their charter bus. "We had a ball," says Mike's brother Kevin. They watched movies and sang songs. The men played cards and dominoes. Leroy Sr. sat in the back. After a while, the kids grabbed the PA microphone on the bus and put on a talent show. The merry travelers pulled into Atlanta on Friday.

The Night before the Game

Between practice, meetings, and media demands, Mike didn't have all that much time to spend with his family. But he did have dinner with about eight family members at the team hotel Saturday night before excusing himself for a team meeting.

Before the meeting, several Rams players, Mike included, were sitting around a table, talking about restaurants. Mike recalls that defensive tackle D'Marco Farr told the group: *"You know there's a guy from San Francisco who made one big tackle in his whole career in the Super Bowl. Now he's got a restaurant people go to just because he made that tackle."*

Vermeil took a matter-of-fact approach in his comments to the squad the night before the Super Bowl. "He went over the whole season,"

Mike recalls. "He told us what got us here and what would win the Super Bowl for us. He reminded us of what we did against Tennessee the last time we played them, how we dug ourselves in a hole but fought our way back. But he reminded us that we were on a neutral field now, and we played them pretty much to a standstill at their place. He said, 'If we don't turn the ball over, we're going to win the game.'"

Vermeil got emotional only when introducing guest speaker Randy Cross, who once played for Vermeil at UCLA and now works as a football analyst for CBS Sports. "We don't know who's going to make the play Sunday," Cross told the Rams. "Who's going to make the play that decides this Super Bowl?"

Cross then talked about an unsung linebacker who helped San Francisco win its first Super Bowl in 1981. (Cross was speaking from experience because he had been a member of that championship team.) The linebacker's name was Dan Bunz, and he now owns a restaurant. At this, Mike looked at Farr, who was grinning broadly. *I told you, Mike. I told you,* Farr said.

Bunz had made one of the greatest defensive plays in Super Bowl history, stopping Cincinnati running back Charles Alexander just inches from the goal line in the third quarter of

Super Bowl XVI. Many of the Rams went to sleep that night wondering who was going to be the next Dan Bunz. Who would make the play to win the Super Bowl? Mike fell asleep around midnight. He slept pretty well.

Game Day

The next morning, Mike made a quick trip to Leslie's hotel to say hello, then returned to eat breakfast with the team. There was a morning meeting to review the game plan, but there was also time to kill. During the regular season, 15 of the Rams' 16 games started at noon. Super Bowl XXXIV wouldn't start until nearly 5:30 P.M.

After the meeting, Mike went back to the room to relax. He watched some TV, napped for about a half-hour, then attended the team chapel service. Mike asked God to help him use the talent he had been given to its highest level in the Super Bowl. He prayed that he and the Rams would play smart football and that no one would get hurt. Then it was time to head to the Georgia Dome.

"I wasn't overly excited for some reason," Mike says. "When I went onto the field for pregame (warm-up), it felt like it was another game." That feeling stayed with Mike for much of the evening.

"The NFC championship game seemed more exciting than the Super Bowl, probably because we were playing at home and our fans were so into it," Mike says. In Georgia, it seemed like more than half the fans were rooting for Tennessee.

The locker room was very calm before kickoff. Mike listened to his gospel CD. Ray Agnew said the pregame prayer. "It was a little more quiet than usual," Mike recalls. "Everyone was just so focused and ready to play."

Mike looked around the room one last time before game time. He saw determination, purpose, and intense concentration in the eyes of his teammates. The Rams were locked in; they were primed for the task at hand. Suddenly, Mike got the same feeling that came over him the Friday before playing San Francisco in Game 4 of the regular season.

We've got this game won," Mike remembers saying to himself. But the Titans, obviously, would have other plans.

As Mike waited in the tunnel to take the field, his thoughts were on a far different task—not losing control when he ran onto the field. Unlike most games, only the Rams' starting offensive unit was introduced before the game, so Mike simply ran out with the rest of the squad after the offense was introduced. Mike rates this as one of the most exciting moments of his career.

What was going through his mind as he sprinted onto the field? Believe it or not, Joe Kelly. Kelly was a former teammate of Mike's with the Raiders. He had played in a Super Bowl for Cincinnati. Mike recalled watching a Super Bowl highlight film of that game and seeing Kelly in a totally hyper state. Because Kelly looked so out of sorts, Mike had asked him, *"What was wrong with you that day?"*

Mike remembers that Kelly told him, *"I was so excited, I had to get oxygen because I started hyperventilating."*

So as Mike raced onto the field with his teammates, he consciously told himself: *"Okay, Mike, whatever you do, calm down. You don't want to start hyperventilating like Joe Kelly."*

Mike didn't. "But I can see why Joe did because when you're in that tunnel right before the game starts, that's probably one of the most exciting feelings you'll ever have," Mike says. "You always have anxiety before the game starts, but multiply that by like 100 before the Super Bowl. Your heart's racing; there's no feeling like it."

One piece of unfinished business remained before kickoff. As defensive team captain, Mike strode out to midfield for the coin toss along with offensive captain Kurt Warner and special teams captain Tony Horne. The Rams' trio was so nervous, so hyped up, no one wanted to call the coin toss.

Finally, Horne said, *"Mike, you're the oldest. You've got to call it."* Mike called "heads," the Rams won the toss, and they elected to receive.

Tired Titans

For every football player, particularly a defensive player, there's always a period of anxiety and nervousness at the start of the game before you participate in your first play. "Once you get past that, then it's just a game," Mike says. "You don't even realize people are there watching you."

Mike's anxiety lasted awhile because the Rams' offense held the ball for nearly 5½ minutes on the opening drive. Mike didn't make his first tackle until midway through the first quarter.

"For some reason, I thought [Frank] Wycheck was hurting on that first drive," Mike says, referring to the Tennessee tight end. "He just wasn't moving like he usually does." Then Mike figured it out. The Titans were tired. They hadn't looked all that energetic in pregame. Mike had even mentioned this to Titans cornerback Steve Jackson before the game.

Jackson told Mike that Tennessee was playing in its 14th straight game without a week off. The Titans regular-season bye had come before their Halloween matchup with the Rams in Nashville. Since then, Tennessee had played every week, including three emotional games in the AFC playoffs against Buffalo, Indianapolis, and Jacksonville. The Rams had the benefit of a first-round playoff bye. They'd also rested most of their starters in the second half of the regular-season finale against Philadelphia.

The Titans may have been sluggish, but the Rams couldn't put them away in the first half. The Rams dominated statistically, outgaining Tennessee by a whopping 294 yards to 89, but they had only a 9–0 lead at intermission. Every time the Rams got close to the end zone, they misfired and had to settle for a field goal attempt instead of a touchdown.

"At halftime, we're kind of upset because we know the game shouldn't even be close," Mike says. "If we're up 17–0 or something, Tennessee's completely out of it at halftime. Then they have to start doing stuff that they're not accustomed to doing."

But it looked like the game had reached that point of no return midway through the third quarter when Warner found Torry Holt in the end zone for a nine-yard TD pass and a 16–0 Rams lead.

Change in Momentum

To climb back into the contest from their third-quarter deficit, Tennessee would have to open up their offense. Throw the ball down field. Take chances. Or so the Rams thought.

"They come out and just play smashmouth football," Mike says. "The first five or six plays [of their first third-quarter drive], we're on our heels. We're thinking *pass*; everyone's thinking *pass*. Instead, they're coming right at us. Eddie [George] caught fire. He started running the ball really hard. They just had everything rolling."

Still, the defense wasn't overly concerned when George capped a 16-play drive with a 1-yard TD run off the left guard. Instead of kicking the extra point, Tennessee tried a 2-point conversion play and failed. So the Rams led 16–6 after three quarters of football.

But the St. Louis offense, which had moved the ball all evening, went three plays and out on their next possession. Tennessee got the ball right back, and like the steady *drip, drip, drip* of a faucet, kept nudging the ball down the field. The Titans picked up three first downs without gaining more than 9 yards on any one play and moved into Rams territory once again.

"We started getting discouraged because we knew we had opportunities to stop them, but we weren't very good on third down," Mike says.

The Titans then reached the doorstep of the end zone with a pair of 21-yard pass plays. George, a big, physical back, finished off the drive with a 2-yard TD run around the right end. Suddenly, the Rams lead had shrunk to 16–13 with 7:21 remaining in the game.

The St. Louis sideline grew quiet. "People were wondering what was going on," Mike says. "The whole season, we had played from ahead on everybody. We had never let anybody back into the game." But that's exactly what was happening this time. The Rams went three-and-out again. Worse yet, Tennessee took over with excellent field position on its own 47 after a short punt by Mike Horan.

The Titans kept pounding away at the Rams' run defense with George. This time the drive stalled on the St. Louis 25. Out came the Tennessee field goal unit. Al Del Greco may have missed the cat food commercial, but he didn't miss this kick. His 43-yarder tied the game at 16 with only 2:12 to play.

Nail-Biting Time

If you think Mike and the Rams were concerned as the game wound down, you should have seen Mike's relatives in the stands. Brother Kevin spent much of the second half out of his seat in a designated smoking area of the Georgia Dome.

"I try not to smoke cigarettes too much, but I guess I smoked a pack of cigarettes in that second half," Kevin says. "I was going through the Salems like nobody's business. But then I said a prayer. Something finally came over me. I said, 'Kevin, it's in God's hands. Quit worrying about it.' "

Sitting in a different section of the stadium, with her parents and Mike's parents, Leslie said a different kind of prayer. While Leslie prays before each game, her prayers don't involve the score, but rather a request for protection—no injuries on either side. After all, it's silly to think that God has a rooting interest in a sporting event. But she couldn't help herself as the fourth quarter ticked away and the Titans crept closer. Leslie knew Tennessee fans were more than likely offering up similar prayers for their team, but she dropped all pretense of neutrality. Her fourth-quarter prayers went something like this:

Dear God, I know You did not bring us this far to let us taste defeat. You wouldn't let us have this Cinderella year for us to get here and lose the game.

After Tennessee tied the score, Mike sat down on the bench and had a perfect view of what happened next. On first and 10 from the St. Louis 27, Warner threw deep to Isaac Bruce.

"Isaac caught the ball maybe 10 yards from where I'm sitting," Mike says. "I can see it all. When I see him catch the ball, I'm like, *'He's going to score!'* That's the first thing that came to my mind. I saw him come back to the ball, and you know how Isaac is. If he makes the first guy miss, there aren't too many guys that are going to catch him. And if the next guy doesn't make the tackle, he's gone."

Which is pretty much what happened. Titans cornerback Denard Walker fell down as Bruce came back to the ball. Titans safety Anthony Dorsett couldn't catch up. Bruce raced 73 yards for a dramatic touchdown.

"I could see all our people standing up on the sidelines," Mike says. "They're jumping up and down. I'm still sitting on the bench, thinking, *'I've got to catch my breath and get ready to go right back out on the field.'*"

That lightening bolt of a pass play had given the Rams a 23–16 lead with 1:54 to play. But Mike knew there still was work to be done. For the second week in a row, it would be up to the Rams' defense to preserve a victory. For the second week in a row, they would be tested to the limit.

The Final Drive

A Titans penalty on the kickoff pushed the ball back to the Tennessee 12. Only 1:48 remained in the game—108 ticks of the clock—and Tennessee had only one timeout left

"If we get the ball back, it's over," Rams defensive coordinator Peter Giunta says. "They can stop the clock only once, and we can just fall on the ball. We know that's the case going into the last drive."

Which made the Rams play more conservative than normal on defense. They didn't want to give up the big play or get caught out of position by trying something risky. Besides, the Rams' defensive unit was dead tired.

Since that Warner-to-Holt touchdown pass midway through the third quarter, Tennessee had run 33 plays, the Rams only seven. The Rams' defense had been on the field for 18:26 of the 20:16 of clock time. "We were exhausted," linebacker London Fletcher recalls.

From the stands, Mary Jo Jones saw a telltale sign that her son was fatigued. "You can tell Mike is tired when he puts those hands on his hips," she says. Such was the case. Worse yet, Mike's ankle was killing him. It had been hurting since midway through the fourth quarter when a teammate accidentally stepped on his foot just before George's second touchdown. Nonetheless, Mike was thinking positive thoughts when he trotted out to the field for Tennessee's last-ditch drive.

"I thought maybe they'd get four, five, six plays, and then we'd stop them and end the game," Mike says.

It took a lot more than that to end the game. It took the most frantic, memorable finish in Super Bowl history. Let's go inside the film room to watch the final drive.

- 1st and 10, Tennessee 12: Rams linebacker Charlie Clemons has inside responsibility. Instead, he chases George to the flat on a pass play. Titans quarterback Steve McNair throws over the middle, right to the space vacated by Clemons, to Derrick Mason for a 9-yard gain. The clock is running.

- 2nd and 1, Tennessee 21: The Rams are in man-to-man coverage with their safeties playing deep. This gives Mike sole responsibility for covering Wycheck, the Titans' tight end. Wycheck catches a short pass for a 7-yard gain and a first down. More important, he slips a tackle by Mike near the sideline and is able to get out of bounds, stopping the clock with 1:20 left. Wycheck no longer looks hurt or tired.

- 1st and 10, Tennessee 28: Rams safety Billy Jenkins does such a good job of "jamming" Wycheck on the play that he moves him right into McNair's throwing lane. As a result, McNair has to throw over Jenkins and Wycheck to get it to Kevin Dyson, which causes an off-target pass. McNair throws incomplete to Dyson. The clock stops with 1:16 to play.

- 2nd and 10, Tennessee 28: McNair makes a nifty scramble to his left, leaving Rams defensive end Grant Wistrom grasping at air as McNair runs down field for a 12-yard gain. Farr, the Rams' defensive tackle, is practically pulled to the ground by a Tennessee blocker, but no holding penalty is called. There is a flag on the play, but it's against Rams cornerback Dre' Bly for grabbing McNair's facemask. Fifteen yards is tacked onto McNair's run. The Titans suddenly are in Rams territory with 1:05 to play.

- 1st and 10, St. Louis 45: With the Rams in a three-man rush, Clemons jumps offside for a five-yard penalty.

- 1st and 5, St. Louis 40: Another three-man rush with the safeties deep and the other six defenders fanned out underneath in coverage. McNair has no place to throw and is almost sacked by Kevin Carter before scrambling out of bounds for a two-yard gain with 49 seconds to play.

- 2nd and 3, St. Louis 38: McNair throws underneath the coverage to Dyson for a 7-yard gain. Farr is tackled, not blocked, on the play by a Titans lineman. Umpire Ron Botchan appears to be looking right at Farr and the Titans player on the play, but there is no flag. The clock is running.

- 1st and 10, St. Louis 31: McNair purposely spikes the ball to stop the clock with 31 seconds remaining.

- 2nd and 10, St. Louis 31: McNair throws toward Mason over the middle. Bly closes fast for an interception but drops the ball. The play is negated by a neutral zone infraction against Carter, a five-yard penalty.

- 2nd and 5, St. Louis 26: The Rams send Clemons to the left and Mike up the middle on blitzes. With the pass rush closing in, McNair gets rid of the ball so quickly that it strikes George from behind. The incomplete pass stops the clock with 22 seconds to play.

- 3rd and 5, St. Louis 26: This is an incredible McNair scramble play, culminating in a 16-yard pass completion to Dyson. Actually, the intended receiver was Wycheck, not Dyson. The Titans had planned a little trickery. McNair was to throw over the middle to Wycheck, who would then lateral the ball back to George, who would be trailing from behind. Yes, it was the old hook-and-ladder play. There was just one problem for Tennessee: The Rams knew it was coming.

"We had practiced against that play all week," Mike says. "We took it away from them." Mike smothered Wycheck; Bly ran step for step with George. With nowhere to throw the football, McNair pumped and started scrambling. Suddenly, pass-rushers Carter and Jay Williams were all over him. Just when it looked like Carter was about to drop McNair, Williams collided with Carter, McNair wriggled free, and he completed the pass to Dyson.

"We took the play away from McNair," Mike says. "We did everything we were supposed to, and he still makes a great play."

The Rams, in fact, did everything right except *have enough players on the field.* Incredibly, the Rams had only 10 players on the field for that play. There were supposed to be two linebackers on the field, but in a personnel mix-up, Mike was the only linebacker out there.

For much of the game, Clemons had been the second linebacker in the Rams' nickel package. At least until Tennessee reached the red zone (the Rams' 20 yard line). Then Fletcher, who has better pass coverage skills than Clemons, would come in to the game. This play started on the St. Louis 26, just outside the red zone, but neither Clemons nor Fletcher was on the field.

After this mad scramble, the Titans used their final timeout. So with 6 seconds left in the game, Super Bowl XXXIV had come down to one play. If the Rams kept Tennessee out of the end zone, they would win. If they didn't, we would witness the first overtime in Super Bowl history.

The Chess Match

"Nickel. 4–3 Blast. Cover 77."

On the final play of the Super Bowl, the basic defensive formation for the Rams called for five defensive backs, a four-man front, and combination man-to-man coverage.

It was *exactly* what the Titans were expecting. Tennessee came out of the huddle with a play specifically designed for it—a play the

Titans had practiced all week.

"In the huddle, I don't think anybody had any doubt in their minds that we weren't about to go in and score," says Dyson, the Tennessee receiver. "We had been doing that all year long, being in close games and pulling them out."

- Flanked to the left for Tennessee were receivers Chris Sanders and Derrick Mason. Sanders was on the extreme left with Mason inside of Sanders—or in the "slot." George also was to the left of the formation but in the backfield. The Rams countered with Bly, who had man-to-man responsibilities on Sanders; cornerback Todd Lyght and free safety Keith Lyle, who double-teamed the inside receiver (Mason); and linebacker London Fletcher, who shadowed George.

- Flanked to the right for Tennessee were Wycheck to the extreme right and Dyson in the slot. Mike had inside responsibility, which meant he covered whichever receiver headed inside. Cornerback Dexter McCleon had outside responsibility, which meant he covered whichever receiver headed outside. Stationed behind Mike and McCleon in a support position was Jenkins at strong safety.

- As usual, the left side of the line featured Carter at defensive end and Farr at defensive tackle. On the right side, however, Jeff Zgonina was in for Ray Agnew, and Leonard Little, normally a linebacker, was in at end.

Zgonina had been a super sub all year, so his presence on the field was no big surprise. The same can't be said for Little, who had done little but play special teams when he played. But both Wistrom and Williams were worn out, so Giunta went with Little.

"Fresh legs," Giunta explains. "We thought we'd try a speed-rush guy coming off McNair's backside. If anybody was fresh on the sideline it was Leonard."

In the trenches, the Rams' defensive ends were simply instructed to go after McNair. They were given a "free" rush. The defensive tackles, on the other hand, were told to "spy" on McNair. In other words, they were to initiate contact with the Titans offensive linemen but keep an eye on McNair to prevent a scramble up the middle. The play would begin on the Rams' 10, so McNair was very capable of darting up the middle to score.

Scant seconds before the ball was snapped, Dyson went in motion to his left. Mike had turned away from the line of scrimmage to hear

Jenkins make a call and didn't see Dyson at first. There was a split-second of panic. "If Tennessee snaps the ball right there, we're in big trouble," Mike says.

With Dyson in motion, the Rams' coverage changed from man-to-man to a zone concept. But instead of continuing to his left down the line of scrimmage, Dyson reversed his tracks and headed to the right, back toward Wycheck. This caused the Rams to switch calls again.

In perhaps 5 seconds, the Rams changed their coverage call from man to zone and then back to man. All before the ball was snapped.

The Snap

With McNair dropping back to pass, Carter got decent pressure at left end. But on the right side, Little went right at Tennessee offensive tackle Brad Hopkins instead of trying to loop around him. He was quickly neutralized.

At tackle, Zgonina stayed in good position, actually dropping off the line of scrimmage a couple of yards to spy on McNair. Despite getting double-teamed, Farr got a good inside push, basically forcing McNair to release the ball. "He didn't want to get caught holding the ball," Giunta says.

Wycheck headed straight down field on his pattern. After coming back in motion toward

Wycheck, Dyson looped around to the outside. Because Mike had inside responsibility, he covered Wycheck. "I thought they were going to go to Wycheck," Mike says. "He's the guy they went to the game before, in the AFC championship against Jacksonville."

If anything, Mike covered Wycheck a little *too* tightly. This made it all the more difficult for Mike to adjust to what happened next.

All along, Dyson was engaged in a cat-and-mouse game with Mike. As soon as Mike committed to covering Wycheck, Dyson thought he was home free. Dyson cut back inside, to a w-i-d-e open middle of the field. McCleon yelled, *"In! In! In!"* signaling to Mike that Dyson had changed directions and was now Mike's responsibility. But Mike didn't hear McCleon. McNair released the ball, and the pass headed toward Dyson. Not Wycheck.

The moment of truth in Super Bowl XXXIV was at hand.

Making the Play

McNair threw a perfect pass, low and right in the stomach. Dyson caught the ball just inside the 5 yard line and headed for the end zone. But by then, Mike already had planted, changed directions, and was headed toward Dyson. Despite covering Wycheck, Mike had been looking "through" the Titans tight end toward Dyson.

"You can tell when a receiver's about to get a ball," Mike says. "Their mannerisms are a whole lot different than when they're not getting the ball. They've got to look back. They've got to turn their head. And they've got to get their hands ready for the ball.

"I'm looking at Dyson, and I can see his eyes get bigger. And I can see him looking back for the ball."

Mike lunged at Dyson and got his right hand around Dyson's waist. "I get a good wrap on him initially with my right arm, but his momentum swings me all the way around," Mike says.

At 6-foot, 2-inches, 200 pounds, Dyson is no toothpick, and he threatened to run through Mike's tackle. But Mike got his left hand around Dyson's shin, just above his left ankle. And down went Dyson!

"He got my feet," Dyson says. "When the feet stop moving, the body stops moving."

Dyson made a late lunge for the goal line, but clearly he had been stopped about 1½ yards short of the end zone. "I was hoping they were going to review the play," Dyson says. "That's why I did that."

The officials were slow to make a call, which concerned Mike. "They kind of hesitated," Mike says. "I knew Dyson hadn't scored, but I'm hoping they hadn't messed up, thinking that he wasn't down and had reached over and got the touchdown."

But with some encouragement from Zgonina, who had been waving off the play near the goal line, officials ruled that Dyson hadn't scored. Dyson rolled over just in time to see the scoreboard clock go from 0:01 to 0:00. Time had expired. The game was over. The Rams had won the Super Bowl.

Mike hopped up and hugged Zgonina and Lyle. Confetti fell from the roof of the Georgia Dome. Dozens of workers rushed onto the field to set up for the postgame ceremonies. Then Mike just stood there for what seemed like an eternity.

Mike remembers that Lorenzo Styles ran up and shouted: *"We won the Super Bowl!"*

But Mike just stood there. *"Are you all right?"* he remembers Styles asking.

"Yeah, I'm all right," Mike answered.

"Are you sure you're all right?" Styles asked again.

Mike just stood there. He wasn't moving. He didn't say anything. And he was tired.

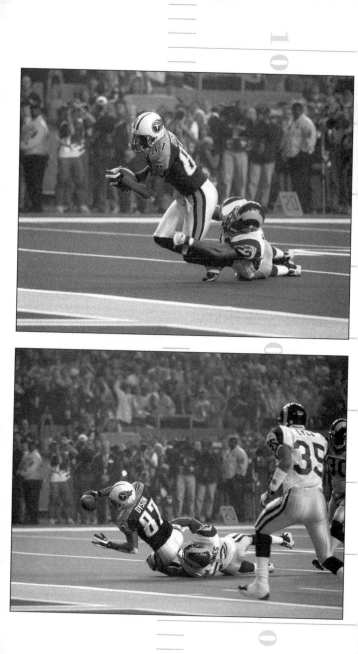

The Tackle: *Regarded as the greatest defensive play in Super Bowl history, Mike Jones secures the Rams' Championship by stopping Tennessee Titan receiver Kevin Dyson at the 1-yard line.*

12

Life After The Tackle

Perhaps a minute passed after The Tackle before Mike snapped out of his trance. There were people everywhere on the field. Mike didn't know who they were. The stage for the on-the-field postgame show had been assembled in an instant. He was vaguely aware of a heated discussion between ABC, which had televised the game, and NFL Security concerning including Mike in the postgame festivities. ABC wanted Mike on the platform; NFL Security said no because there were already too many people onstage. In the end, ABC's Lessley Visser pulled Mike aside for a quick interview, as did ESPN.

Then Mike saw Leslie and his mom. They weren't permitted on the field, but Mike always knows where they're sitting, regardless of the stadium. They talked for just a moment. *"We finally did it!"* Mike told them.

Then he headed to the locker room. Interestingly, it was an alcohol-free locker room—none of the champagne-squirting hi-jinks that you normally see after a major sports championship. Mike briefly exchanged hugs and congratulations with a few teammates and coaches. Ray Agnew said the postgame prayer. Then Mike headed into the training room to have his ankle checked out. It was just a bad sprain.

Next, Mike was summoned to a media podium. He talked for 20 to 25 minutes before a crowd of reporters. The recurring answer from Mike when asked about The Tackle? *"It was just a tackle to me. I was just doing my job."*

By the time Mike showered and dressed, the locker room was deserted. "If I wasn't the last person out, I was probably the second-last," he remembers. He boarded a bus headed to the hotel for the team party. Leslie rode along. Upon arriving at the hotel, he did interviews for CBS and for ESPN's "Up Close." With all the immediate media interest in Mike, the magnitude of The Tackle was clear to everyone, it seemed, but Mike. "You know what? It wasn't sinking in to be honest with you," Mike admits.

At the team party, held in a packed hotel ballroom, Mike probably sat down for all of five minutes. Joined by most of his family, at least those old enough to stay up after midnight, Mike posed for what seemed to be a zillion photos. Everyone in the room—or close to it—came up to congratulate him. Leslie stuck a chicken wing in his hand to give him something to munch on. And although not much of a dancer—remember, this is the guy who had trouble with the Bob & Weave—Mike took to the floor with Leslie and other family members, sore ankle and all.

Several players had talked about going out on the town, but Mike never made it. It was easily 4 in the morning, and Mike wanted to pack before going to sleep. Bags had to be in the hotel lobby by 6 A.M. Mike slept all of one hour before waking at 6:30 to do a radio interview. The team left for the Atlanta airport at 8:30 A.M.

Welcome Home

Back in St. Louis, Mike and Leslie and a few others went out to lunch, then it was time to head downtown for the victory parade. The team assembled at the Kiel Center—home of the hockey Blues—where they boarded the parade vehicles. It was cold and getting dark by the time the parade finally started. After about a quarter mile, they turned down Market Street— one of the major thoroughfares of downtown St. Louis—and headed toward Kiener Plaza, a small urban park in the shadow of the Gateway Arch.

It was then—and only then—that the Rams players, coaches, and wives realized the magnitude of the crowd. A quarter of a million people had braved the winter evening to express their love and admiration for the hometown team.

"That was so unreal," Leslie says. "We turned the corner to go down Market, and it was amazing. They had been out there in the cold. Waiting. You knew the Rams had fans, you knew that the fans loved them, but it was just incredible."

It was St. Louis' way of saying thanks. The Rams had gone from 4–12 in 1998 to Super Bowl champions the following season. It was the biggest one-year turnaround in the history of the National Football League.

The next day, Mike and Leslie heard a radio announcement concerning a major press conference scheduled that afternoon at Rams Park. No other details were available; and Mike had no inside information. But Mike immediately turned to Leslie and said, *"Coach Vermeil's about to retire."*

Mike didn't have time for a long good-bye at the press conference. He had to fly to New York that night for a two-day interview extravaganza. The off-season whirlwind was officially underway.

He did the *Regis & Kathie Lee Show.* Both

were nice, but Regis mistakenly called Mike "Mike Woods" on the air. Then Mike appeared on the *Charlie Rose Show,* did an interview segment for HBO's *Inside the NFL,* and was quizzed by CNBC. He was a featured guest at the All-Star Café. He did a few radio and TV interviews for local stations. More important, he found time to take Leslie to the Broadway production of *Cats.*

On the Go

As the off-season progressed, Mike never slowed down. He taped a TV public service announcement for the 2000 Census ... served as co-chair of an AIDS charity walk ... was a featured speaker at the 100 Black Men national convention in Newark, New Jersey ... spoke at numerous schools ... appeared in numerous charity golf tournaments ... and on and on.

Prior to the Super Bowl, Marci Moran and the Rams' community relations department received 10 to 15 requests a week for player appearances. After the Super Bowl, those requests tripled, and they kept pouring in long after the Rams claimed the Lombardi Trophy. "We're getting slammed," Moran said in May, nearly four months after the Super Bowl. "We can't keep up with the demand."

Nearly four months after The Tackle,

requests for public appearances by Mike kept pouring in. "He hasn't been on the cover of *Sports Illustrated*," Moran says. "But in this town, I think he's right up there with Kurt [Warner]. People love to have Mike Jones out— love it. And when he goes out, he gets rave reviews.

"One thing that's definitely changed for Mike now is that people know who he is nationally. Before it was like Isaac Bruce, Marshall Faulk, Kurt Warner. But with the Super Bowl, Mike has really jumped up. People know he made the game-saving tackle. Everybody knows who he is just because of that one play."

Super Bowl heroics often can bring post-Super Bowl endorsements. "But that's not even the issue with Mike," Moran says. "He was so excited about The Tackle and all the notoriety he's gotten because he knew it would help his foundation. That's why he was happy about it."

The Michael Jones Foundation has indeed flourished since The Tackle. Attendance at Mike's football camps is setting all-time highs. Sponsorship is no longer a problem. Former NFL players who once turned Mike down when asked to help at one of his camps are now saying yes. Revenue from the foundation's St. Louis golf tournament and dinner auction alone were in excess of $100,000 in the spring of 2000. At the dinner auction, an autographed Warner jersey went for $800, but an autographed Mike Jones jersey brought in $1,800.

Mike was so busy on the charity front that he really didn't try to maximize endorsement opportunities. "Mike's picky," says agent Harold Lewis. "He knows what he wants, and he knows what he doesn't want to do. A lot of things that we turned down, he just didn't believe in. There was one guy that wanted us to do a speaking commercial for $10,000 about a divorce attorney."

Mike said no thanks. But he did agree to numerous speaking engagements and signing appearances. Many of those honorariums were donated to the foundation. His $7,500 speaker's fee at the 100 Black Men convention in June, for example, went straight to the foundation. His proceeds from this book will also go to the foundation.

Victory 2000

One of Mike's more unique postseason appearances took place in a familiar setting—the Trans World Dome. The atmosphere was electric; the decibel level rarely louder. Thousands watched the exploits of Mike Jones, Kurt Warner, defensive end Kevin Carter, and tight end Ernie Conwell on the floor of the dome. Was this another celebration of the Rams' championship run?

Nope. It was Victory 2000—more than a celebration of the Rams' march to the Super Bowl, it was a celebration of these four players' faith in Jesus Christ and an opportunity to share with others the many ways God is active in their lives.

More than 25,000 spectators attended—young and old, black and white, religious and non-religious. Nothing like this had ever been attempted before by professional athletes, at least not on such a grand scale. Warner was the Victory 2000 organizer, and St. Louis area churches covered expenses to rent the dome and host the event.

It was a no-brainer for Warner to ask Mike to be one of the night's featured speakers. "He's a strong Christian," Warner says. "That's definitely what we were looking for, first of all. But beyond that, we were looking for guys that were big leaders on the football team, as well as in the community. Guys that people around St. Louis and around the area could really grab hold of. Mike is a perfect example of that.

"We hoped that would give credibility to what we were doing in Victory 2000 because he is so highly looked upon both by players around the league and, I think, people in this community. He's exactly what we were looking for. A guy that people would stand up and listen to, not just because he plays football but because of all the other things he does."

In between sets of contemporary Christian music, which had the dome jumping like any concert, the four Rams players shared their faith with the crowd. Carter talked about how his faith helped him overcome injuries and maximize his football talent over the last two seasons. Conwell also talked about his long road back from a major knee injury in 1998. "It took a lot of strength to get through it," he told the crowd. "I'm here to tell you that I couldn't have done it on my own. "God loves you. I'm here tell you."

The featured speaker was Warner. He talked about his rise from grocery-shelf stock boy to Super Bowl MVP. "The reason I tell you this is because it hasn't always been great," Warner told the crowd. "I haven't always been the Super Bowl MVP. I haven't always been the NFL MVP. That's just this last season. I've had my ups, and I've had my downs."

When Warner finished telling the crowd how the Lord had worked and continued to work in his life, replays of The Tackle began to flash on huge video screens behind the stage. The crowd energetically welcomed Mike to the stage. "Last year, I was having some troubles," Mike told the crowd, referring to his troublesome 1998 season. "And I think the troubles stemmed from me not letting things go. As you can see, I'm not the biggest. I'm not the fastest. I'm not the strongest person to play in the NFL. You could say some of the same things about David in David and Goliath.

"If you have some trouble in your heart, leave it up to God. He'll take care of it. You may not be the biggest or the fastest or the strongest, but God will …"

Be there to help you tackle life's problems. And as Mike will be the first to tell you, God is there in the midst of questions about the future, raising children, marriage difficulties, doors shut in your face, financial worries, and career challenges. And God is also there in the midst of the many successes, whether they are personal or professional victories.

Mike would later say that his comments were totally impromptu. No script. No rehearsal. No artificial ingredients added. "I didn't know what I was going to say until I got up on stage," he says. "I just cut it loose. Let it fly." He put it in God's hands, just like he does each day of his life, each time he steps on the football field.

Victory 2000 was a big success, and Warner

& Co. are thinking of doing it again, perhaps in another city. "I think it was important for us to do something like that," Mike says. "Even if you weren't Christian, you got something out of it that you could use constructively in your life. That's what you always want to try to do, just point people in the right direction."

Still On the Go

Mike always has been the type of person who likes to have several things going at once. "My wife always says I like chaos," he explains. "I'm always in constant motion."

Life after The Tackle has made the chaos even more, uh, chaotic. "It's hard for Mike to say no," Leslie admits. "So that makes it even worse. He likes disarray anyway. He doesn't like to plan. He likes to go by the spur of the moment. He'll have a meeting downtown and then one way out in the suburbs. Why not try to schedule meetings that are closer together on the same day? But he likes it that way."

At first, all the activities were fun for Leslie. She tried to keep up. But as her pregnancy advanced, she grew tired more easily. Finally, she told Mike he was on his own. "It was at least two or three things each week," she says. "It took its toll on me."

Leslie also worried that it would take its toll

on Mike—that he would never slow down in the off-season, meaning he wouldn't recharge his body and mind for training camp. "That's what I've been fussing with him about," Leslie says. "I don't think he had an opportunity to have down time. I really don't. He's been on the go, on the go, on the go. I've tried fussing: 'You need to tell them no. Don't schedule anything this week. At least have a day off.'"

But that didn't happen often. "What I should have done in the first place is put it in the Lord's hands," Leslie says. "He'll see to it that Michael gets the rest that he needs. I think Michael's looking forward to training camp because nobody can get to him there. He can't make any appearances there."

Better yet, there are no cell phones on the practice field, and none are allowed in the team meeting rooms. Despite his hectic schedule, Mike missed only a couple of days during the Rams' off-season conditioning program. But it might be a first that a player actually looks forward to training camp for rest, relaxation, and peace of mind.

"I'm always usually busy in the off-season, but you add winning the Super Bowl, and now you multiply it by 10," Mike says. "It can wear on you at times because people want you to do so many different things."

Even when Mike is "off the clock," so to speak, it doesn't necessarily mean he can enjoy private time with Leslie and Ashley. A lot more people recognize Mike in public these days. "We used to be able to get through dinner without people saying, 'There's the guy that made The Tackle. Can I have your autograph?'" Leslie says. "I'm not used to sharing him that much with everybody, and that's what I'm having to adjust to."

We Meet Again

One person who didn't recognize Mike—before or after The Tackle—was Tennessee Titans wide receiver Kevin Dyson. That is not until a visit to Rams Park a little more than three months after the Super Bowl.

Dyson graciously agreed to visit the enemy's lair as part of a magazine article about The Tackle that would appear in *The Sporting News.* Dyson, Mike, and writer/editor Dennis Dillon had dinner together the night before they viewed the game film. Prior to that get-together, Dyson confesses, "I didn't know what Mike looked like."

The next day, Dyson sat in a meeting room with Mike, watched game film of The Tackle, and broke down the play. The film review session was fascinating. For Dyson, it marked the first time he had watched the play—and The Tackle—since the day after the Super Bowl. As the weeks passed, friends told him what a memorable game it had been and urged him to watch it on tape. Dyson did so—except for the final 6 seconds.

"I didn't watch that part," Dyson says. "I just stopped the tape."

Even on a spring day in May some 16 weeks after the fact, it was painful for Dyson to finally view the play again. "It's not to the point where it's devastating," Dyson says. "But it is the Super Bowl—to get so far and be so short. We drive 87 yards, and we're a yard short. That's not the last memory you want to have going into the off-season."

But Dyson sat in that film room at Rams Park for more than an hour with Mike, replaying The Tackle over and over and over. Could Dyson have done anything differently on the play? "Maybe if I cut my route a little flatter [made a sharper cut to the middle], I might have been able to outrun him to the end zone," Dyson suggests.

At first, Mike agreed with that assessment. But after looking at the play several more times, he changed his mind. "You know what? I'm looking at you the whole time," Mike says. "If you do that, I'm coming right down on you anyway."

But there's absolutely no doubt that Mike was the only player on the field even close to being in position to make the play. "The middle of the field was so open," Dyson points out. "If Mike wasn't there, I would have walked into the end zone."

Before the session broke up, Mike and Dyson agreed to a playful game of "what if." What if Dyson had dropped the ball? "I probably wouldn't be in the league right now," Dyson says, drawing laughter.

What if Mike had missed the tackle? "I'd probably be living back in Kansas City right now," Mike says, drawing even more laughter.

But what if Dyson gets in the end zone somehow? What happens in overtime? "Hopefully we win the toss, get the ball first, and we do what we did in the whole fourth quarter," Dyson says. "Try to run them to death."

"I tell you one thing, we didn't want it to go into overtime," Mike admits.

The Road Ahead

The college running back that nobody wanted on draft day will play his 10th NFL season in 2000. It's the last year of Mike's original four-year deal with the Rams. He wants to play through one more contract. "I think as long as I keep myself in shape and I don't have any injuries, I can play four or five more years," Mike says. He'd like to make a Pro Bowl. "That's the last piece of the puzzle."

And Mike would like to retire as a Ram. "We won the Super Bowl here," he says. "There were so many things we went through as a team, as players. It built a lot of camaraderie. We can still do some good things. I think we have a good chance of defending our title, and defending it for a couple years, because we've got a lot of young players in the prime of their careers."

Although Mike is nearing the end of his career, he figures he can always do better. He can improve as a pass rusher. He can make more tackles. He can even improve on his Super Bowl performance. Instead of making the game-saving tackle, why not score the *game-winning* touchdown in Super Bowl XXXV?

Mike likes the sound of that. "Yeah, that might work," he says.

But even if he never makes another tackle, even if the Rams never make another Super Bowl, no one can take away what they accomplished during the 1999 season. "It was said that you couldn't win with good people, but even our stars are unselfish," Ray Agnew points out.

So what about the old axiom that nice guys finish last? "Not this time," Agnew says. "Not this time."

Small-World Department: One of Dyson's college coaches at Utah—Fred Whittingham— was Mike's linebacker coach in 1995 and 1996 with the Raiders. Whittingham and Dyson spoke not too long after the Super Bowl. "He told me Mike was one of the surest tacklers he ever had," Dyson says. The entire football world knows that now.

Postscript

In the frantic weeks after the Super Bowl, Mike didn't run into teammate D'Marco Farr until March. When they finally spoke for the first time since the game, Farr reminded Mike of Dan Bunz, that big tackle for San Francisco in Super Bowl XVI, and the restaurant with Bunz' name.

"So when does your restaurant open, Mike?" Farr asked.

Not that I have already obtained all this,
or have already been made perfect,
but I press on to take hold of that for
which Christ Jesus took hold of me.

Philippians 3:12

Photo courtesy of Bill Stover, photographer, St. Louis.